J O H N
MACQUARRIE,

a Master of Theology

John Macquarrie (left) with theologian Karl Rahner in front of

Christchurch, Oxford, two weeks before Rahner's death in 1984.

J O H N
MACQUARRIE,

a Master of Theology

Owen F. Cummings

FOREWORD BY
John Macquarrie

Paulist Press
New York/Mahwah, N.J.

All photos are courtesy of John Macquarrie

Cover design & interior design by Lynn Else

Library of Congress Cataloging-in-Publication Data

Cummings, Owen F.
    John Macquarrie, a master of theology / Owen F. Cummings ; foreword by
John Macquarrie.
      p. cm.
    Includes bibliographical references and index.
    ISBN 0-8091-4071-3 (alk. paper)
    1. Macquarrie, John. I. Title.

BX4827.M25 C86 2002
230'.044'092—dc21

                              2001059117

Published by Paulist Press
997 Macarthur Boulevard
Mahwah, New Jersey 07430

www.paulistpress.com

Printed and bound in the
United States of America

Table of Contents

Table of Contents

Table of Contents

FOR
John Macquarrie

Foreword

It is both a pleasure and an honour to write this brief foreword to the truly excellent book of Owen Cummings. He and I come from the Glasgow area of Scotland, and we both owe much to that city's university, celebrating this year the 550th anniversary of its foundation. It was only long after we had both left Glasgow that we met and soon became fast friends. Although the author describes me as a "master" of theology, I have told him that we are both "students" of the subject. What has happened is that theology has mastered both of us, so that we have been caught up in the lifelong task and joy of seeking better to understand, expound and respond to the Christian vision of life.

I am myself coming near to the end of my theological career, whereas Owen is still near the beginning. It is a great encouragement to an older theologian when he learns that some younger man or woman has found his work of sufficient interest to write about it. I can say that my thought has been accurately expounded in this book. Owen has been appreciative but not uncritical. A theologian understands his own thought better when someone else writes about it. Even criticisms show where the argument has been weak or badly expressed, and call for further thought on particular topics. It is in this way that the theological enterprise may hope to advance. That enterprise is not in the hands of individuals, but is a collegiate undertaking within the body of Christ. Each learns from the other; we are all of us both teachers and learners.

Though the book is primarily about my own theological thinking, it is a witness to the power and maturity of Owen's theological strength and promises further valuable contributions from him.

John Macquarrie

CHAPTER 1

Introducing
John Macquarrie

"Theology may be defined as the study which, through participation in and reflection upon a religious faith, seeks to express the
content of this faith in the clearest and most coherent language available."[1] This is how John Macquarrie describes theology. It is equally
revealing of the man himself. His lifelong commitment to the theological enterprise begins with participation in a religious faith. He
has never been a thinker who reflects on Christianity from a distance, but always from the within of the Christian community and
tradition. Through a theological contribution that has been critically
constructive, always courteous, even with positions and insights with
which he finds himself in disagreement, John Macquarrie has put his
life at the service of the Christian faith throughout much of the
twentieth century, and now into the twenty-first. This chapter will
attempt to provide some insight into the man and a brief overview
of his principal theological publications in chronological order.

Early Life and Education

John Macquarrie was born on June 27, 1919, in Renfrew,
Scotland, the only child of John and Robina (née McInnes)
Macquarrie. His parents had married in 1914 and they had a son
who died in infancy. His mother told him that he himself barely sur-
vived. Macquarrie's grandfather, a Gaelic speaker, had come from the
Island of Islay, off the west coast of Scotland, to work on Clydeside.

John Macquarrie, a Master of Theology

His family was not poor but they were certainly not affluent. His father worked in the shipbuilding industry as a pattern maker. Though it was a skilled occupation, he would not have earned more than three pounds per week. Both his parents were very devout, his father being an elder in the Presbyterian Church, but Macquarrie says of himself that he never had *what might be called a conversion experience.* Commenting on his religious background, Eugene T. Long writes:

> Macquarrie's upbringing fostered in him a sense of deep religious commitment that has always been balanced by tolerance and an openness toward others. He recognized early both the importance of religious conviction and the legitimacy of religious diversity. Indeed, both a spirit of charity and a depth of conviction equally characterize his work.[2]

Long has been a student of Macquarrie's, both directly and indirectly, since the 1950s, and his characterization of Macquarrie is both entirely accurate and also one of the most attractive features of his thought.

Reflecting on his initial interest in the ministry and theology, Macquarrie notes that motives are always mixed. He describes positively the influence of a minister in his hometown of Renfrew: *I think to some extent a bit of hero worship comes into it. Our pastor at the time was a man of considerable learning who had a first-class degree in philosophy, who practiced what he preached.* At the same time, *being a minister of the Kirk was quite a nice position in society.* The minimum stipend which most ministers of the Church of Scotland received was about three hundred pounds a year along with a house. Although there was no dramatic moment when he received a call to the ministry, the first time he recalls being conscious of the ministry as a personal vocation was when he completed an application form for Glasgow University. He had been studying the normal range of high school subjects at Paisley Grammar School, and in the fifth year of the course he entered and won a Glasgow University bursary competition. It was worth forty-seven pounds a year, adding almost another pound to the weekly household budget, and without it he probably would not have gone to university. Part of the university application form inquired about the candidate's vocational aspirations, and Macquarrie found himself writing "the Christian ministry." He began his university education at the University of Glasgow in 1936, receiving his first degree, the M.A., with first-class honors in mental philosophy in 1940.[3] He was a student of Charles Arthur Campbell, professor of logic and rhetoric, to whom in 1972 he dedicated his book *Existentialism*.

F. H. Bradley and C. A. Campbell

Among all the philosophers he studied "the one who really bowled (him) over" was F. H. Bradley (1846–1924), who had been a fellow of Merton College, Oxford.[4] Bradley's *Appearance and Reality* had a considerable influence on him, a work described by the anonymous author in *The Oxford Dictionary of the Christian Church* as "the most original work in British metaphysics in the 19th century."[5] Subsequently, Macquarrie was to describe Bradley in equally positive terms: "…undoubtedly the most brilliant of the neo-idealists and probably the greatest British philosopher of any school in recent times."[6] Although standing loosely in the Hegelian tradition, Bradley differed from Hegel:

> Hegel was, to use the technical term, panlogist, so that the real was the rational and the rational was the real. Bradley was more of a mystic. The Absolute for him—he did not speak so much of God as of the Absolute—is the ultimate reality and is suprarational. It is beyond our grasp. This became a kind of mystical element in his philosophy. But he also thought that the study of metaphysics is the way in which a lot of people experience religion. The Absolute is the Whole and for Bradley "God" is not the form of the Absolute. "God" is, as it were, this side of the Absolute. God, shall we say, is a kind of rationalized version of the Absolute.

John Macquarrie, a Master of Theology

Macquarrie finds a passage in Bradley's *Principles of Logic* particularly revealing. While we were discussing how Bradley's philosophy influenced him, he left his study and disappeared up a ladder into the attic of his home, where his library is now stored, found the particular passage immediately, and read it to me:

> Suppose (let us say) a man convinced of the truth of Christianity and rightly or wrongly to understand Christianity as the unity of God with finite souls, a reality at once consummated and eternal and yet temporal and progressive. Christianity is to such a man a main aspect of the Universe, conscious of itself above time, and yet revealing itself in the historical growth of spiritual experience. And imagine the same man asked to compare with this principle the truth about some happening in time. I will not instance such events as the virgin birth and bodily ascension of Jesus of Nazareth, but I will take the historical assertion that Jesus actually at a certain time lived and taught in Galilee and actually died at Jerusalem on the cross. And by "actually" I mean so that, if *we* had been there, we should have seen these things happen. "All such events," our supposed man might reply, are, if you view them as occurrences, of little importance. Enquire by all means whether and how far there is good evidence for their happening. But do not imagine that Christianity is vitally concerned with the result of your enquiry. Christianity, as I conceive it, covers so much ground, fills such a space in the Universe, and makes such a difference to the world, that, without it, the world would be not so much changed as destroyed. And it counts for much that this eternal truth should have happened on our planet (as presumably elsewhere), and should here (we hope) be developing itself more and more fully. But the rest, if you will take it as mere event and occurrence, is an affair so small—a matter grounded by the very nature of its world on

so little—that between the two things there can be hardly a comparison.[7]

Here is a large panoramic vision of reality that stands in clear contrast with a narrow religious vision, even though it fails to appreciate the importance of history. Macquarrie says of this passage that: *It made a big impression on me. I don't hold it nowadays because I do think that historical truth is important. I changed my mind about that.* It is rather tempting to see in Macquarrie's summation of Bradley's metaphysics his own self-reflection when he writes, "The aim of metaphysics is to satisfy the intellect. The intellect is satisfied only by that which is one and free from contradiction; this is *reality*."[8]

He sees the idealist tradition of Bradley continued in his own teacher, C. A. Campbell. In his discussion of Campbell again it is not difficult to see Macquarrie's own image. Outlining Campbell's appropriation of Rudolf Otto's doctrine of the numinous, Macquarrie concludes:

> This means that our language about God is not literally applicable, but is symbolic of a reality which is in itself unknown. But if our talk of God is not to be utterly empty, we would need to suppose that there is some affinity between our symbols and what they symbolize....Campbell argues further that the symbolical knowledge of God of which he speaks is no more agnostic, it would seem, than the knowledge permitted by scholastic philosophy's doctrine of analogy.[9]

We see here in his observations of Bradley and Campbell some of the characteristics of his own mature theology, the need and importance of metaphysics in theology and the care with which language must be used of God.

Theology and Ministry

Macquarrie then proceeded to the study of theology also at the University of Glasgow, then housed at Trinity College, a magnificent structure looking down upon Charing Cross and Sauchiehall Street. During his years at Trinity College, Macquarrie worked at the parish church of Dumbarton, and for two years helped to start a new congregation in Paisley. The town had experienced an increase in the worker population in a wartime factory, but Macquarrie "being somewhat introverted and shy," apparently did not find this work particularly satisfying.[10] In theology while he found biblical criticism and church history interesting, he disliked systematic theology, especially Calvin and Barth. A course offered on Buddhism by Dr. A. J. Gossip also interested him, as well as a course on Islam by Dr. James Robson. He was awarded the degree of B.D. in 1943 and was offered a scholarship to do further theological studies at Westminster College, Cambridge. He declined the offer and served in the British Army as a chaplain from 1945 to 1948. As an army chaplain, Macquarrie's principal responsibility was the oversight of German prisoner-of-war camps in the Middle East. He shares one interesting experience from this time. In London, in a transit center waiting to board a ship for Egypt, he tells of an experience that made a lasting impression on him, his first experience of Benediction of the Blessed Sacrament in St. Andrew's Anglican Church, Willesden Green:

> The bell was summoning the people, and I went in. The first part of the service was familiar to me, for it was Evensong, with its splendid collects and canticles, its psalms and readings from Scripture. But then followed something new to me, though I had indeed read about it and was able to understand what was going on—Benediction of the Blessed Sacrament. No doubt I was in an impressionable mood that night, but this service meant a great deal to me. Evensong had already meant much, but now, as it were, an additional dimension was also opened up. I did not know what lay

ahead of me or when I might come back to these shores again, but I had been assured of our Lord's presence and had received his sacramental blessing....Looking back, I do not think I am wrong in seeing in this incident a step on the way by which God, in his merciful providence, was calling me into the fullness of Christian faith and worship.[11]

In the essay from which this extract has been taken, Macquarrie offers a most commendable apologia for Benediction. Later, Macquarrie's eucharistic theology was to undergo considerable development, but that is to anticipate what will be dealt with in a subsequent chapter.

This experience that Macquarrie relates fits with the description he gives of his "naturally religious temperament":

With me "religion" is not a bad word....By "religion" I mean an awareness of the holy, of the depth and mystery of existence. It can be a sense of presence, or, paradoxically, a sense of absence. Perhaps it is part of my Celtic heritage, for it is very close to the sense of presence which John Baillie described, and which he said he had had from the beginning of his life and which he took to be the main root of belief in God. Like Baillie too, I thought of this mystery in terms of immanence rather than transcendence.[12]

After army service, Macquarrie became the minister of St. Ninian's Church, Brechin, in 1948. He was to remain in Brechin until 1953. In 1949 he married Jenny Welsh, and they have three children, two boys and a girl: John Michael, Catherine Elizabeth, and Alan Denis. During his time at Brechin, as the result of a suggestion made by a former theology professor from Glasgow, Dr. J. G. Riddell, he embarked on theological research and completed his Ph.D. in theology under the supervision of Ian Henderson (1910–69), who was among the first to introduce the work of Rudolf Bultmann to the English-speaking world, with his book *Myth in the New Testament*.[13]

His doctoral dissertation, a comparison of Rudolf Bultmann and Martin Heidegger, was to be published as *An Existentialist Theology* in 1955, dedicated to his parents. From the preface to *An Existentialist Theology,* we are given a sense of the scope of the work: "...the right of the apologist to make use of current philosophical concepts; the claim that there is a special relation between the philosophy of existence and the work of theology; and an affinity between the concepts of existentialism and those of biblical thought."[14] Macquarrie speaks warmly of Henderson in the preface, and in a later essay, published after his death, considers Henderson "in the first rank of Scottish theologians of this century."[15] In 1953, one year before completing the dissertation, Macquarrie began his academic career as a colleague of Henderson's, as lecturer in systematic theology at the University of Glasgow. The next ten years or so represent Macquarrie's "existentialist phase."

Lecturer at the University of Glasgow

In 1956, Ronald Gregor Smith (1913–68) joined the Glasgow divinity faculty as Primarius Professor of Divinity. Gregor Smith, as editor of the Student Christian Movement Press, had been responsible for a new series of publications, the Library of Theology and Philosophy, and Macquarrie's *An Existentialist Theology* was the first volume. He was six years Macquarrie's senior, and the two men make an interesting contrast.

Gregor Smith was born in Edinburgh, son of a marine biologist, Macquarrie in Glasgow, son of a Clydeside shipyard craftsman. Gregor Smith graduated from the University of Edinburgh, first with an M.A. in English language and literature (1934) and then with a B.D. (1937), Macquarrie from the University of Glasgow with an M.A. in mental philosophy, and then the B.D. As Macquarrie (in conjunction with E. Robinson) was to translate into English Martin Heidegger's *Being and Time,* so Gregor Smith translated Martin Buber's *I and Thou.*[16] Both of them, however, were keenly interested in Rudolf Bultmann. One commentator on Gregor Smith writes:"If there was one theologian to whom he was most indebted both intellectually and personally it was Rudolf Bultmann."[17] Both Gregor Smith and Macquarrie could be said to have been in their existentialist phase in Glasgow together, though unfortunately there grew an estrangement between Gregor Smith and Ian Henderson. Probably the most outstanding expression of the joint work of Macquarrie and Gregor Smith during their Glasgow years was their joint supervision of the doctoral dissertation of Eugene Thomas Long, a comparison of Rudolf Bultmann and Karl Jaspers.[18] Both Gregor Smith and Macquarrie were to develop in quite distinct theological directions, the former decisively influenced by "secular Christianity" informed in various ways by Dietrich Bonhoeffer and Friedrich Gogarten, the latter moving in a decisively Anglo-Catholic direction both ecclesiologically and doctrinally, so much so that the Scottish Presbyterian theologian Alasdair Heron was to describe him in 1980 as "perhaps the leading Anglican theologian of the present day."[19] Of Macquarrie Gregor Smith says: "...[he] has done much to restore philosophical theology to a position of reasoned assurance in recent times."[20] Discussing Gregor Smith's "secular theology," Macquarrie remarks that

> At the end of his life, the late Ronald Gregor Smith was struggling with the question of God. He was in violent reaction against classical theism, and especially against the notion of an unchanging God, throned above the chances and changes of time. Though a secular theologian—and he understood that to mean an historicizing theologian—he did not run away from the God question, as many of the secularizers did.[21]

Both men remained critically aware and appreciative of each other's theology.

Another well-known member of the divinity faculty at this time was the popular New Testament scholar, William Barclay (1907–78), who was a minister in Renfrew when Macquarrie was a boy. He is described by Macquarrie *as an old-fashioned liberal, an evangelical minus the fundamentalism*. Although Macquarrie is mentioned a number of times in Barclay's authorized biography, we are not given any sense of relationship between them, though Macquarrie speaks of him fondly.[22] Theologically there would have been serious differences between them, Macquarrie with an increasingly Catholic ecclesiology, Barclay an evangelical free churchman by conviction.

We are given a different insight into John Macquarrie in the reminiscence of a Scottish Jesuit spiritual theologian, Gerard W. Hughes. Hughes, who had been brought up in Glasgow, completed his theological formation at the Jesuit Faculty of Theology in Frankfurt. Expressing an interest in Scottish theology after his ordination to the priesthood, Hughes inquired among his Glasgow Jesuit colleagues about their contact with Church of Scotland ministers. The reminiscence is best given in his own words:

> They had none, so I went to the Church of Scotland office and asked to see their directory of clergy in Glasgow. I found the divinity faculty at Glasgow University, took a phone number at random and arranged to meet a lecturer, John Macquarrie, with whom I had two three-hour sessions, which ended with supper in the kitchen with his wife and himself. John Macquarrie was far better read in Catholic theology than I, yet he had never in his life spoken with a Catholic priest....I was delighted to meet him again after fifteen years when Glasgow University gave him an honorary doctorate.[23]

Although Hughes is not explicit, it seems from the Catholic representatives in his *Twentieth Century Religious Thought* that Macquarrie was probably reading people like Karl Rahner, Romano Guardini, and Hans Urs Von Balthasar.

Union Theological Seminary

Macquarrie took up a post at Union Theological Seminary in New York City in 1962, having first delivered the Hastie Lectures at the University of Glasgow on "The Problem of Theological Language." Along with other essays, papers, and lectures given in the United States there came *God-Talk: An Examination of the Language and Logic of Theology* (1962). His 1962 inaugural lecture at Union was entitled, "How Is Theology Possible?" That year also saw his translation, along with Edward Robinson of the University of Kansas, of Martin Heidegger's *Sein und Zeit*.[24] In 1963, at the invitation of the editorial staff of Harper and Brothers he published his *Twentieth Century Religious Thought,* dedicated to his three children. The ferment in theology at the time made such a book invaluable to the student of theology trying to understand how to take the pulse of theological pluralism in the early 1960s. Macquarrie realized the magnitude of the task that he had been invited to assume, but in his typically humble way, he wrote in the preface: "At first I shied away from so wide and laborious an undertaking. But on reflection, it occurred to me that if I were to make the attempt—and surely someone ought to make it—then even if no one else were to profit from my book, I should at least educate myself a little better in writing it."[25] In this book, acclaimed almost universally for its even handedness and fairness so much so that it has been issued in an updated form three times (in 1971, 1981, and 2001), he outlines and critically responds to over one hundred and fifty philosophers and theologians. Eugene T. Long says of this book that it "testifies to Macquarrie's responsibility to sum up the essential aspects of a theory or system of thought in a few words. Macquarrie's critical commentary also provides a guide to the maturation and development of his own thought."[26] Hard on its heels in 1966 came his *Principles of Christian Theology,* in which he draws heavily on Heidegger's philosophy as a vehicle through which to express the tradition of Christian doctrine. However, in this much-used and applauded book he moves decisively out of an existentialist mold into what he calls the "existential-ontological" method.

The 1960s witnessed some radical movements in theology, especially the "Death of God" theology associated with Thomas J. J. Altizer, William Hamilton, and Paul M. van Buren. Forms of secular or religionless Christianity advocated by Harvey G. Cox and connected with varying degrees of accuracy to Dietrich Bonhoeffer were widespread. In response to such movements, Macquarrie wrote *God and Secularity* (1967). This book, according to his own analysis in "Pilgrimage in Theology," marks a turning point in his theological development. From now on he would turn his attention more and more to articulating the themes of Christian doctrine enunciated in his *Principles of Christian Theology*.

Macquarrie's appointment to Union also brought him into contact with process theology, especially in the person and work of a colleague for whom he had enormous respect, Daniel Day Williams. In an essay written in appreciation of Williams after his premature death, Macquarrie writes that "I was [Williams'] close colleague for eight years, and we often discussed theological questions."[27] Later in his Gifford Lectures, *In Search of Deity,* Macquarrie describes something of their theological relationship:

> [Williams] looked to Whitehead for his categories of theological explanation, while I looked to Heidegger, and we used to compare the merits and demerits of these two philosophers. I had to concede that Whitehead provided a much more adequate theology of nature, but Williams in turn admitted that Heidegger had the more profound understanding of the human person....[28]

It must be acknowledged that process theologians have found in Macquarrie a sympathetic fellow. This reflects their joint appreciation of the necessity of metaphysics for theology, but also their dynamic views of reality. The late Norman Pittenger, for example, teaching at the Anglican school, General Theological Seminary, during Macquarrie's stay in New York, says that if he did not find the thought of Whitehead and Hartshorne so compelling, he would opt for and endorse the thought of John Macquarrie.[29]

The years at Union Theological Seminary not only chart Macquarrie's theological development, but also his ecclesial affiliation. Macquarrie became a good friend of the Union New Testament scholar John Knox. Shortly after Macquarrie arrived in New York, Knox gave him a copy of his latest book, *The Church and the Reality of Christ,* in which "Christ and the Church comprise together the unity of the Christ-event."[30] Although a Methodist, Knox's developing ecclesiology was taking him in another direction and, in fact, in December 1962, he was ordained a priest in the Anglican Communion. Macquarrie's theological pilgrimage was taking him in the same direction too, and so in January 1965 he was ordained deacon and in June priest in the Anglican Communion by Bishop Horace Donegan of New York. Macquarrie dedicated his *Principles of Christian Theology* to John Knox, mentioning in the preface his indebtedness to Knox's "profound insights into the nature of the Church."

University of Oxford

In the autumn of 1970, Macquarrie returned to the United Kingdom to become the Lady Margaret Professor of Divinity in the University of Oxford. The chair went with a canonry of Christ Church Cathedral and a large mansion of over thirty rooms in the heart of the college, and it is said that the Macquarries made rooms in the house available to students whose financial means made it difficult to find appropriate accommodation in Oxford.

Macquarrie succeeded in the Lady Margaret Chair Frank Leslie Cross (1900–68), the patristic scholar, best known as convenor of the First International Conference on Patristic Studies in 1951 and editor of *The Oxford Dictionary of the Christian Church.* Macquarrie held this chair until 1986, when he in turn was succeeded by Rowan D.

Williams, another scholar whose competence reached into the patristic tradition as well as into contemporary Orthodox theology.

Since his return to the United Kingdom, a stream of books on different aspects of Christian doctrine has poured from Macquarrie's pen. *Paths in Spirituality* (1972) was devoted to prayer, worship, and spirituality. In the new edition of this book published in 1992, there are three additional chapters: "Eucharistic Sacrifice," "The Reconciliation of a Penitent," and "Rest and Restlessness in Christian Spirituality." *Three Issues in Ethics* (1970) is taken up with moral theology. *Christian Unity and Christian Diversity* (1975) demonstrates his interest in and commitment to ecumenism, and William Green remarks of this book that "Macquarrie takes up John Knox's argument that the Roman Catholic Church must be the center of visible unity."[31] He suggests that church unity might be structured after the pattern of the Uniate Churches, a pattern that allows communion with Rome as well as a measure of self-determination and autonomy. Contemporary dissatisfaction with uniatism as an ecumenical method might put his approach in a different light, but it would not seem to deflect from his central conviction that the only realistic approach to healing past divisions is some form of unity with Rome, but without absorption. Particular issues in the *Quaestiones disputatae* chapters of the book have been further refined by Macquarrie, especially his understanding of the Blessed Virgin Mary and the Petrine Ministry. *Christian Hope* (1978) develops Macquarrie's approach to eschatology. Beginning with a phenomenology of human hope in general terms, he goes on to outline the history of eschatology before making his own proposals for a contemporary understanding. In terms of individual eschatology, his central conviction is that if God is indeed as he is manifest in the person of Jesus Christ, he could not permit death to wipe out his care for his personal creatures. *The Faith of the People of God* (1972), a fine example of a systematic theologian writing for a nonspecialist audience, *Thinking About God* (1975), a collection of essays and papers that finds its focus in a more organic relationship between God and the world and eschews a spectatorial or monarchic image

of God, and *The Humility of God* (1978), a series of provocative med-
itations on the articles of the Creed—all wide-ranging explorations
of Christian doctrine and Christian theologians. In 1977 he published a revised edition of his *Principles of Christian Theology*, about
which he writes: "The fundamental teachings remain unaltered, but
there is a good deal of new material, also clarifications and explanations to meet the criticisms of (Alistair) Kee and (Huw Parri) Owen
particularly, though I have not actually named them....The new edition has some fresh material on most topics...."[32] William Green
provides a most useful summary of the principal areas of doctrine
that have been supplemented in this revised edition:

> (1) The philosophical criticisms of natural theology have
> been expanded and separated from the theological ones, and
> a more affirmative stance taken toward traditional natural
> theology; (2) there is less emphasis on human finitude and
> more on the inborn drive toward human transcendence; (3)
> greater balance has been given to the treatment of the per-
> son and work of Christ; (4) consideration of the Blessed
> Virgin is now supplemented by positive statements regard-
> ing her immaculate conception and assumption; (5) the
> concept of "ministerial collegiality" makes its appearance for
> the first time.[33]

Beginning in the 1980s, Macquarrie took up various themes
from the *Principles* for yet further development and exploration. *In
Search of Humanity* (1982) offers an account of his anthropology that
goes well beyond the anthropology of the *Principles*. For example,
there are chapters on "Embodiedness," "Love," "Art," and "Hope" as
well as aspects of an existentialist anthropology so well represented
in *Principles*. As he works through the many and various elements of
what it means to be human, an important ingredient in his understanding is dialectic: willingness to enter as far as one can into mutually opposing systems of thought or action in order to find and, if
possible, reconcile the insights on both sides. This is vintage

Macquarrie and is taken further in respect to God in the next book. *In Search of Deity* (1985), his Gifford Lectures in the University of St. Andrews, takes further his interest in natural theology, in which Macquarrie demonstrates his progression from the "panentheism" of his earlier work to "dialectical theism." As he articulates his dialectical theism, he considers a series of contrasts about God: knowability and incomprehensibility, transcendence and immanence, impassibility and passibility, eternity and temporality. In his careful treatment of these opposites, Macquarrie comes close to paradox as the least inadequate way to speak of God. *Theology, Church and Ministry* (1986) gathers up a wide range of contemporary and, at times, controverted topics that reflect the title, for example: "Pride in the Church," "The Meeting of Religions in the Modern World: Opportunities and Dangers," "The Bishop and the Theologian," and "The Ordination of Women to the Priesthood." In the essay, "The Bishop and the Theologian," Macquarrie reflects on the importance of theology to the ministry of the bishop, something to which he returns even more emphatically in his recent *A Guide to the Sacraments*.

Retirement

In retirement, John Macquarrie has continued to be prolific. *Jesus Christ in Modern Thought* (1990), which won the HarperCollins Religious Book Prize, represents his mature Christology. For years, apart from the synthetic treatment of *Principles,* Macquarrie has been putting out papers reflecting different issues in Christology. Thus, he has written on such diverse Christological topics as "The Humility of God"; responses to the British *The Myth of God Incarnate* debate in the late 1970s: "Kenoticism Reconsidered," "Tradition, Truth and Christology," "The Humanity of Christ," to name but a few. The 1990 book brings all this material together in an ordered fashion. The first part of the book deals with the New Testament sources of Christology, the emergence of classical Christology, and its development through the Reformation. In the second part, he plots a trajectory through modern Christology, all of which prepares for the third part, his own contemporary expression of belief in Jesus Christ. In 1998 he published *Christology Revisited,* the Albert Cardinal Meyer Memorial Lectures delivered at Mundelein Seminary in the Archdiocese of Chicago. In his own words, after publishing *Jesus Christ in Modern Thought,* "as soon as the book was finished and fixed in print, I began to realize that some things that might have been said had not been said, that many things could have been said better, while still other things should perhaps not have been said at all."[34] In *Mary for All Christians* (1990), on the encouragement of Dom Alberic Stacpoole, O.S.B., a colleague from Benet Hall, Oxford, Macquarrie published an accessible Mariology, accessible both ecumenically and to the lay reader. In his Hensley-Henson Lectures at Oxford in 1993–94, published as *Heidegger and Christianity* (1994), Macquarrie returns to the work of the philosopher Martin Heidegger. When asked if starting all over again in theology whether Heidegger would still be a central philosophical dialogue partner, Macquarrie answered in the affirmative.

> *I think for various reasons he has never been taken very seriously in England, partly because English philosophy in the last fifty years or so has been very much tied to the analytic tradition. Heidegger combines both analysis and synthesis, and there are theological elements in Heidegger. His view of Being is not unlike Bradley's Absolute, because Heidegger does not equate Being with God. Being is somehow beyond God. You could think of it in various ways as somehow like those early theologians such as Dionysius. Dionysius speaks of the thearchy, beyond divinity. The idea comes up in Tillich too, the "God beyond God." There are depths in God which we simply cannot grasp.*

He notes that even the supposed atheist theologian, Don Cupitt, in his most recent work speaks of the *Fountain,* a term found also in Heidegger.

Being is the Fountain, that which gives itself, that which is the foundation of other things. In his latest books Cupitt talks about the religion of Being, which is very Heideggerian. I don't think Cupitt has sufficiently studied Heidegger, but it seems a more promising line than some of his earlier work. Heidegger says of himself that he is neither a theist nor an atheist, but it depends so much on how these terms are defined. His last essay was an interview which he gave to a journalist from Der Spiegel, *and he called it* "Only a God Can Save Us." *In that essay Heidegger says that we cannot bring God back. There is a mystical element of waiting for God.*

Invitation to Faith (1995) was originally published as *Starting from Scratch: The Nature of Christian Faith,* a series of lectures given in Lent, 1994, in St. Andrew's Church, Old Headington, Oxford. It is a fine example of Christian apologetics, not least because after every chapter, we are provided with some of the ensuing discussion between Macquarrie and the participants. *Mediators Between Human and Divine* (1996) brings him back to something in which he has been interested since his B.D. days in Glasgow, the great religious traditions of the world. Finally, *A Guide to the Sacraments* (1997), which grew out of lectures at Nashotah House in July of 1996 and which is thoroughly ecumenical in character, brings us up to date with the published theology of John Macquarrie.

Evaluations and Responses

In anyone's theological journey some theologians will figure more centrally than others. For me John Macquarrie has been the paradigm of mature Christian theology and a constant reading companion since 1968. Not everyone, however, will find his theology equally attractive and appealing. Balanced, critical accounts may be had in James J. Bacik, *Contemporary Theologians,*[35] and Daniel W. Hardy, "British Theologies: Theology Through Philosophy."[36] Bacik, a Catholic theologian who did his doctoral work on Karl Rahner under Macquarrie at Oxford, offers a most positive assessment of his supervisor: "Macquarrie has been a most valuable guide precisely because of his balance, clarity and respect for tradition. His creative work is solid because it is deeply rooted in a long and diverse tradition."[37] In the preface to his doctoral dissertation, Bacik again acknowledges Macquarrie's theological scholarship: "His great breadth of scholarship and fine human sensitivity are impressive to me...."[38] Hardy, an Anglican theologian, is more critical. He shows "the steady development" in Macquarrie's theology from the influence of Bradley, through his existentialism to his comprehensive systematic theology. Hardy points to a certain tension "between a general religious faith and the particular claims of Christian faith."[39] Hardy's judgment seems right here. Macquarrie certainly refuses to isolate Christian faith from an innate and universal human religiosity, but equally he takes with great seriousness the objective fabric of Christian doctrine. There is an unavoidable tension here, and Macquarrie's chosen theological methodology refuses to dissolve it in favor of the one or the other, general religious faith or the specificity of Christian faith.

In the first edition of his justly celebrated synthesis of Catholic doctrine, *Catholicism,* Richard P. McBrien compares his project to Macquarrie's *Principles of Christian Theology:*

> The final product...is slightly more akin to Anglican theologian John Macquarrie's *Principles of Christian Theology...* than to Catholic theologian Hans Kung's *On Being a Christian....*Macquarrie's work deliberately seeks a balance between what Macquarrie calls the existentialist and the ontological approaches to Christian theology: the one emphasizing the personal and the subjective, the other emphasizing the essential and the objective.[40]

One has the impression that the way in which McBrien has shaped *Catholicism* owes not a little to Macquarrie's inspiration, and in the new edition published in 1994, one will find over thirteen references to various aspects of Macquarrie's theology. One could go on adding to the list of theologians who have been influenced or helped by Macquarrie, and such references abound in his *Festschrift*. Singling out these references and testimonies has but one purpose, that is, to establish something of the warm ecumenical appreciation of Macquarrie's work. Whatever individual differences one might have with specific aspects of his theology, the words that constantly come to mind in describing his contribution are: scholarship, sensitivity, balance, respect.

However, one especially stinging reaction to Macquarrie's work came from the pen of the late Donald M. Mackinnon, a Scottish theologian teaching at Cambridge. Stories, often embellished, abound about Mackinnon, and his theology has been helpful to many. The Methodist theologian, the Rev. Professor Frances M. Young of the University of Birmingham, in her moving account of personal pain and suffering as she struggled with a severely handicapped son, is a witness to Mackinnon's penetrating lectures on the problem of evil. By way of contrast to superficial treatments of theodicy, he demanded clear and conscious engagement with the sheer horror of evil.[41] In a similar way, the late Dr. Robert Runcie, former Archbishop of Canterbury, attended lectures by Mackinnon when he was a student at Oxford. The benefit was real albeit not immediate. Runcie says, "If you took down what Donald said, you couldn't understand it at the time, but you gradually worked your way into something which was really significant."[42] Again, the Catholic theologian, Professor Nicholas L. A. Lash, Mackinnon's successor in the Norris-Hulse Chair of Divinity at Cambridge, testifies to Mackinnon's influence as a teacher: "That Christian theology discovers and maintains its peculiar *akribeia* only in the measure that philosophy is 'complicated' by agony is, I think, amongst the more important lessons that Donald Mackinnon has helped me to learn."[43] Nonetheless, there was an unnecessarily acerbic side to Mackinnon. In a lengthy review of Macquarrie's *Studies in Christian Existentialism*, Mackinnon begins:

> Students of contemporary theology must welcome the appearance of this collection of essays by Professor John

Macquarrie, as they provide an excellent introduction to the tendencies of which he is a very influential spokesman. He is a lively, if often superficial writer, self-confident, repetitive, likely to prove very persuasive to those who, through lack of the proper philosophical equipment, may be tempted to find in his favoured nostrums an intellectual panacea.[44]

He goes on to contrast Macquarrie most unfavorably with Hans Urs von Balthasar, a theologian whose work was congenial to Mackinnon and whose then untranslated *Herrlichkeit* he was introducing to the English theology-reading public. Describing his own philosophical bias as "impenitently realist," Mackinnon goes on to suggest that Macquarrie "needs (and I must add that a careful study of his over-praised *Twentieth Century Religious Thought* abundantly confirms this) to deepen and enlarge his philosophical perceptions." Even allowing for the strong contrast that Mackinnon wishes to draw between Macquarrie's theology and his own, this is unduly harsh and destructive. The Scottish Dominican theologian, Father Fergus Kerr, who was a student of Mackinnon's at the University of Aberdeen, makes some interesting remarks apropos of the idealist-realist debate that help to throw light on Mackinnon's views. Kerr notes that in the mid-fifties Mackinnon's insistence on what he took to be "realism" was well established, but "A decade later his attitude to tendencies that he detected in modern theology had greatly hardened."[45] Kerr contextualizes Mackinnon's hardened position, but that cannot justify the rudeness and crudity of expression. About Mackinnon's own style of theology Macquarrie says,

> I must confess that it doesn't appeal particularly to me. It's difficult to know. It's kind of nebulous, and I'm not quite sure what he's on about. Mackinnon was subject to some very strong likes and dislikes. I am not the only victim of his displeasure. John Knox, the New Testament scholar, also fell victim. Mackinnon was quite vicious in that review in the Journal of Theological Studies, *and I remember (Dennis) Nineham saying to me, "That review is*

23

actionable." I don't know if he even bothered to read the book because the review did not touch on the substance of the book at all. The review brought me letters from various people, for example, John N. D. Kelly and Eric L. Mascall, assuring me that Mackinnon's view was not widely shared nor supported. Mascall was quite critical of existentialism—in fact, he thought that Rahner was too much under the spell of Heidegger—but he considered that Mackinnon was wide of the mark in this review.

I pointed out to Macquarrie the contrast between Mackinnon's mean-spirited review and the review of *Principles of Christian Theology* that came from the pen of John N. D. Kelly, the patristic theologian and principal of St. Edmund Hall, Oxford. Kelly describes *Principles* as a "one-volume *Summa*" that demonstrates "a masterly grasp of theological issues and unrivalled clarity of exposition" as its author presents a "highly successful restatement of traditional Christian beliefs within the framework of a new-style natural theology inspired mainly by the writings of Martin Heidegger."[46] Macquarrie then showed me a letter that he received in New York from Kelly before he left for Oxford and the Lady Margaret Chair. In Kelly's letter the following passage may be found:

> Although we both have a Glasgow connection, I do not think that we have ever met, but in spite of this I should like, if I may, to congratulate you on your recent book *Principles of Christian Theology*. I have read this recently with absorbed interest and admiration, and would like to say how impressed I am by your skill at presenting our faith so persuasively in the context of an ontological existentialism....May I also say how distressed I was to read our friend Donald Mackinnon's savage attack on your *Studies in Christian Existentialism* in the recent issue of the *J. T.S.* Some of his comments are grossly unfair, but I suppose we must accept them as examples of the neurotic obsessions which Donald all his life has had from time to time with particu-

lar issues. In any case the review is so unbalanced that I cannot think it will do your work much harm.[47]

The early Mackinnon was greatly influenced by Karl Barth, especially his Christocentrism and the sheer, gratuitous givenness of revelation. Macquarrie, on the other hand, has been rather critical of Barth's theology. He gives a more positive role to the innate human quest for God and to the prereflective or unreflective experience of God as Holy Being. Macquarrie and Mackinnon represent quite contrasting theological viewpoints. Their differing philosophies or metaphysics also come into play. Mackinnon has been consistently critical of Bradley's metaphysics, and it may be, as Fergus Kerr avers, that Mackinnon in his passionate support of realism sought to expose "sometimes with a great ferocity" what he considered to be an idealist tendency in much modern theology, but that will not do. A fierce defense of one's theology or philosophy does not warrant discourtesy either to a text or to a living person. A courteous hearing and a vigorous response seem to be moral requirements in any publicly credible intellectual exchange.

While I was speaking to Macquarrie one morning, he received a phone call from Hong Kong to do with some legal difficulties of copyright in a Chinese translation of one of his books. Pursuing the matter further, he took down from his shelves the Chinese translations of a number of his books. The fact that an English-language theologian is translated into Chinese and Japanese as well as European languages (see the details in the bibliography published in his Festschrift) gives some indication of his accessibility to the believing community and his contribution to the upbuilding of Christian faith. "Reception" by Christian theologians and people is an important hermeneutical principle in "faith seeking understanding." The global reception, both geographically and ecumenically, that John Macquarrie enjoys is more than adequate testimony to his status as an important Christian theologian.

Conclusion

David Tracy has suggested that there are two basic forms of the Christian imagination, the analogical and the dialectical, the former reflecting in the main the Catholic and Orthodox traditions, the latter the Reformation tradition.[48] The analogical imagination tends to emphasize the immanence of God in his creation, the dialectical God's transcendence, but seldom if ever are these shapes of the Christian imagination encountered in a pure form. Although he does not use Tracy's terminology, Macquarrie seems to share his perspective when he writes "Post-Reformation Christianity has, on the whole, stressed God's transcendence at the expense of his immanence."[49] The good theologian, recognizing the infinite complexity of his or her subject matter will acknowledge each form as the corrective of the other. It is a matter of balance as one reverences the Mystery of God and his dealings with us, both-and and not either-or. John Macquarrie, it seems to me, is an excellent example of such balance at work, demonstrating throughout his work a sense of God's immanence and transcendence. He exemplifies both modes of the Christian imagination in fruitful tension. Here is a systematic theologian from whom much may be learned, a theologian described by Louis Bouyer as having "a positive sense of Protestantism," but who is also *très catholicisant*.[50]

CHAPTER 2

Speaking of God

The doctrine of God is central in any Christian account of theology. John Macquarrie's work in theology has coincided with developments and challenges to the received doctrine of God, from the death-of-God theologians of the 1960s, in reference to whom he wrote his *God and Secularity*, to those who are concerned with a critique of classical Christian theism, with which critique he has been engaged from his *Thinking About God* to *In Search of Deity*. This chapter will attend to Macquarrie's understanding of God, both exposition and evaluation, but will necessarily be incomplete until a consideration of his Christology is provided in the following chapter.

God as Holy Being-Letting-Be

How do we speak of God? There is no neutral, no purely objective approach to understanding "God." Everyone pursuant of an understanding of God brings to that quest the story that she or he is. Quite simply, everyone *is* a story, or better, a story made up of countless other stories. Everyone brings to the theological task presuppositions that are emergent from familial, ecclesial, cultural contexts. Everyone is traditioned. We *see* God differently. That is not to say that there is no overlap between one person's seeing and another's, nor that all seeing is of equal value. That form of thoroughgoing relativism is nothing short of performative contradiction. What attracts to one form of seeing over against others, what is appealing about one system of metaphysics rather than another, is that it brings one's reflected experience to a depth of richness and vitality not matched by any alternative. It yields what the Scottish Presbyterian theologian Allan D. Galloway has called *sanitas* or wholeness, "the enjoyment of an integrity of response."[1] Or, changing the philosophical climate in the direction of Bernard Lonergan's brand of transcendental Thomism, a reflected metaphysical position, a reflected seeing of God and God's relations with created reality, is *virtually unconditioned,* that is to say, no other alternative has the capacity satisfactorily to answer all relevant questions with suasive satisfaction.[2]

A theistic system of thinking is very close to what the American Jesuit philosopher W. Norris Clarke calls "a personal psychological predisposition towards metaphysical thinking, something like a *metaphysical bent of mind.*"[3] This predisposition toward metaphysical thinking, according to Clarke, is marked by two qualities: "a passion for unity, for seeing the universe and all things in it fit together as a whole, a longing for integration of thought and life based on the integration of reality itself," and "a sense of some kind of overall hidden harmony of the universe, which could be picked up and possibly spelled out if one listened carefully enough." Although arguably a metaphysics is never complete, since completeness in any Christian interpretation is itself an eschatological condition, a "way of seeing" offers real and sustained nurture to one who wishes to see. Throughout all his writings, John Macquarrie has offered such an integrated, harmonious, theistic way of seeing.

There is another consideration in approaching a Christian understanding of God, and that has to do with the capacity of that understanding to relate to and to integrate with the entire symbol system of the fabric of Christian doctrine. David Tracy writes: "…the full Christian understanding of God occurs only in and through an entire systematic theology encompassing all the great symbols of the tradition."[4] In terms of this criterion Macquarrie has clearly been successful, not only in the systematic vision he presents in *Principles of Christian Theology,* but also in the numerous essays and books since that publication in which he has taken further or refined various doctrinal elements of that systematic vision. In the light of this paragraph, how does John Macquarrie "see" God?

In attempting to answer this question it must be recognized at the outset that while Macquarrie stands clearly within the history of Christian reflection as shall be seen, he is also pushing out the boundaries of this tradition to reach toward a more adequate understanding of God. Writing in 1985, Eugene T. Long summarizes Macquarrie's approach to God:

> Macquarrie shares much with classical theists, yet he argues that we have passed beyond the God of classical theism, that is, beyond the idea of God as a personal being, albeit invisible, bodiless, intangible, who created the world, exercises governance over it, and intervenes on occasions. The need for positing such a God has diminished, he argues, as the scientific capacity to account for the events of the world has grown. Macquarrie has not yet provided a fully developed theory of God to replace the God of classical theism; but he has taken several significant steps in that direction....[5]

This summary of Long's is helpful but requires further nuance. To say that Macquarrie maintains that we have passed beyond "the idea of a personal God" as an aspect of classical theism is somewhat ambiguous. There is no doubt that he does not think of God as *a* being, nor that he expresses concerns about understanding God *exclusively* in personal terms, yet the idea of God as personal remains central to Macquarrie's theology. Again, it is questionable whether Macquarrie feels it is in principle possible to produce "a fully developed theory of God." There is a constant concern throughout his oeuvre to cherish and reverence the transcendent mystery of God in an almost apophatic fashion. Nonetheless, Long seems quite right to say that Macquarrie has taken "several significant steps" to push beyond the God of classical theism.

For Macquarrie, God is "Holy Being," and in so describing God he is adopting and adapting the philosophical categories of Martin

Heidegger. In using this term, "Holy Being," Macquarrie is expressing his existential-ontological concern. God is Being, but Being understood as gracious and responded to by humankind. In order to understand more completely this concept of God it is necessary to ask what exactly is meant by the term "Being."

First, it is useful to say what Being is not. Being is not *a* being. Commenting on Heidegger's concept of being upon which Macquarrie is reliant, Eugene T. Long writes: "Being, according to Heidegger, is not an entity. It is that without which beings would not be and as such cannot itself be a being. It is no-thing from the standpoint of existing entities."[6] Neither is it a property or a quality, and the use of the very word "it" is a concession to the human need for some usable symbol. Being is that which properties and qualities presuppose, and does not as such add anything to an entity. Nor again is Being "substance," because this is static, modeled after thinghood. Finally, Being is not the absolute, if this is taken to mean "the all-inclusive being or as the totality of beings or as the sum of beings."[7]

Since Being is not an entity, nor a property, nor a substance, nor the absolute, it is, strictly speaking, ineffable and incomparable. It is best described in Heidegger's phrasing: "Being is the *transcendens* pure and simple."[8] Being transcends all the categories of our thinking. Does that mean, as some analytic philosophers might suggest, that the word *Being* is meaningless? The answer for Macquarrie is no because Being, or better, Being-letting-be is the response to the question, "Why is there anything rather than nothing?" Of course, there is nothing particularly new in this formulation of the God question. Coming from the standpoint of classical theism, for example, the Dominican theologian Herbert McCabe, using the philosophical theology of St. Thomas Aquinas, argues that "God" is the answer to the question, "Why is there anything rather than nothing?"[9] How McCabe and Macquarrie "see" God is, however, quite different in some respects, but they both share at least the notion that "God" is an heuristic symbol that responds to this basic question arising from the fact of existence.

Not everyone feels the need to ask this ultimate, radical question, "Why is there anything rather than nothing?" This leads to the issue of awareness of Being, a reflexive awareness of Being, or an awareness tending toward reflection. Awareness of Being is not something of which human beings are ordinarily conscious. Frequently, a person has to come up against the nullity of existence in order to be opened to the wonder of Being.

> We only notice this wonder when it is placed over against nothing, but then we see that overcoming nothing and standing out from it is Being, not as something else which exists, but in the sense of that wider being within which all particular beings have their being. Since Being is not another being but the *transcendens,* the incomparable and wholly other source and unity of all beings, it normally escapes our notice.[10]

A person becomes aware of the threat of nonbeing when the precariousness of existence is encountered, and it is death that brings perspective and points beyond being to Being. If one is at all concerned about personal development, growth, and direction in life, it is impossible to avoid thinking about death. This experience is called the "wonder of Being," or the "wonder of wonders" in Heideggerian terminology and seems to be similar to what is expressed in Wittgenstein's words in the *Tractatus Logico-Philosophicus:* "Not *how* the world is, is the mystical but *that* it is."[11]

Although Being is the *transcendens* pure and simple, Being is known only through the beings. In other words, "Being" is a symbol signifying "that which permits the beings to be; that which explains the being of beings. Being lets-be all that is. It is the essence of Being to let-be. And so, all entities in virtue of their existence participate in Being."[12] Another way of putting it is to say that God is the condition that anything may exist, and in so far as something exists, it exists in God. Reflecting on Macquarrie's notion of letting-be as empowering or bringing into being, Yeow Choo Lak puts it like

31

this:"A being *is* in virtue of the fact that it is, but Being is not something that is but lets-be and therefore precedes any is-ness. So, Being is different from beings, yet it is the *spring* and *origin* of all beings; the beings are contingent on and originate from Being."[13] A corollary of this is that we only know God because he lets himself be known, that is, knowledge of God depends on God's letting-be of reality, for it is through things and in things that we are led to the *transcendens.*

In referring to God as Being-that-lets-be, Macquarrie is sharing a perspective in common with other theologians, the perspective which moves from that-which-is-to-be-explained to that-which-explains. Two such theologians are Hywel D. Lewis and James Richmond. Lewis moves from observation of how things are to argue that there must be "some completeness or explanation" to explain all that is.[14] Similarly, Richmond insists that "experience throws us beyond the empirical towards an explanation which is ultimate and absolute."[15] Lewis, Richmond, and others who argue in this vein are referring to the essential "letting-be" quality of Macquarrie's Being.

Not all are in agreement about this manner of proceeding. Keith Ward, for example, maintains in a rigorous analysis that this kind of approach, using the notion of explanation as a base is inadequate. For Ward, "The main problem here is what could be meant by the notion of a comprehensive explanation of everything, or of a self-explanatory being."[16] Because of its obscurity—this *Explicans* precisely because of its ultimacy is inherently and necessarily obscure, that is, "it" itself is by definition unavailable for immediate analysis— Ward thinks that such a self-explanatory being does not really explain anything, is not informative. In other words, to explain the familiar in terms of the incomprehensible is a useless exercise. Since the major purpose of explanations is to help people understand the world better, such an "explanation" is not very helpful. But there may be more than one way to understand and to use the word *explanation*. Perhaps an heuristic reaching out to an answer to the question why anything at all exists instead of nothing is a kind of explanation. Empirically based explanation is obvious enough (at first glance anyway). A bulb is planted, and given the appropriate conditions, a crocus grows. Empirical explanation consists in the elements of soil, plant nutrition, and climate. But why this should be so at all is not open to empirical explanation but to what might be called *metempirical* explanation. It consists in an extrapolation from empirical data to a hypothesis that is variously informed. Being-that-lets-be (or the positions of Lewis and Richmond, among others) is in this class of metempirical explanations. This particular explanation is informed by religious experience, both individual and collective. Ward notes this later in his chapter on "God as the Ground of Being": "Belief in a general rational and moral order cannot plausibly be said to derive by induction from empirical evidence, or from the purely speculative desire to explain the world more fully. It derives from a religious commitment to the moral and purposive ordering of one's experience, in a particular religious tradition."[17] Macquarrie is a theologian sharing in the commitment of religious faith and is engaged in the attempt to articulate systematically its meaning. As such, his talk of Being-letting-be is eminently meaningful within the perspective of the Christian tradition.

Belief in God is faith in Being. "Belief in God is the faith that there is a context of meaning and value that transcends our human life, a context that we do not create and in which we already find ourselves."[18] God is the creative, mysterious ground of our existence and the existence of all reality. To believe in God is to accept reality as trustworthy at the deepest level, to have faith in the worthwhileness of existence even when existence seems absurd. Faith in Being may be for many the basic, implicit, intuitive grasp that life is worth living, or it may flourish in response to Being as holy, a response encountered and nurtured through the givenness of the Christian tradition.

There are three basic criteria for measuring the adequacy of concepts of God in Christian theology. The first is Scripture: Does the concept of God reflect the biblical concepts of God? Second is tradition: Does the concept of God faithfully reflect and represent the triunity of God, the central affirmation about deity in the

Christian tradition? Third is worship or communion with God: Does the concept of God assist and promote deepening awareness of the reality of God in prayer?

The model of God as "Holy Being" is verified in Scripture and throughout the Christian tradition, according to Macquarrie. The classical biblical passage for understanding God as being is Exodus 3.14. The controversy surrounding the precise interpretation of this verse continues, but two things are certain. The Hebrew verb *hyh*/to be—in whatever grammatical form—is the center of the verse, and in Hebrew the verb "to be" includes the verb "to become."[19] In some way, the verb is connected with the is-ness of God. The New Testament lends further corroboration. In St. John's Gospel the words *ego eimi*/I am occur like a refrain (John 6.35; 8.12, 58; 11.25; 15.1). According to Macquarrie, these words are "an unmistakable echo of Exodus."

This tradition was continued through the Fathers into the medieval period. Macquarrie quotes Aquinas in this respect: "Since the being of God is his very essence (which can be said of no other being) it is clear that among names this one (Being/*esse*) most properly names God; for everything is named according to its essence."[20]

The precise ways in which the concept of God as Holy Being can nurture the spiritual life is developed to some extent by Macquarrie in that section of the *Principles of Christian Theology* entitled "Applied Theology" and also in his *Paths in Spirituality*.

The Incomprehensibility of God

Nonetheless, the meaning of "God" is no more exhausted by the language of being than it is by any human language. There is a tendency in human nature to take our ideas of God too literally, almost as if in these ideas we were able to reach God-in-himself. Clearly, Macquarrie considers it illuminating to think of God as Holy Being, that this language has a long and respected tradition behind it, that it is consonant with contemporary philosophies of being, and that it is fundamental or foundational in a way that no other language is.

However, such language needs to be complemented by other ways of talking about God, because God is indefinable and incomprehensible. Nicholas Lash is emphatic throughout his work on this notion of God's incomprehensibility as a perduring conviction of Christian discourse. Thus, he writes in respect of continuity and discontinuity in the Christian understanding of God: "Where continuity is concerned, if I were asked to list those features of Christian discourse concerning God which have recurred most persistently in the course of the church's history, in an impressive variety of social and cultural contexts, one which would come high on my list would be the conviction that it is impossible to understand God."[21] Macquarrie would be in complete agreement with Lash, and so he takes to task theologians who have tended to speak of God almost exclusively in terms of the I-thou encounter. Personal language for God, for Holy Being, is arguably essential for the reason that it best enables relationship in and with God in worship and prayer, but, at the same time, it cannot be denied that like all analogous language for God, personal language is also finally inadequate for understanding the Divine Reality. All human language is finally inadequate because God is not a being but Holy Being. An exclusive personalism tends to make the reality of God no more than a dimension of human existence. The meaning of God is no more exhausted in the terms of personalist philosophy than it is in terms of existential-ontological theism.

The Immanence of God

A more immanentist concept of God is required in which God and the world will not be so sharply separated. Western theological thought has been too much under the dominance of what Macquarrie refers to as the "monarchical" model of God, that is, God understood as absolutely self-sufficient, absolutely transcendent, and for whom the world is external to his own being. Here we come close to the spectrum of views that falls under the heading "process theology," typified in such thinkers as Samuel Alexander, Alfred

North Whitehead, and Charles Hartshorne. While Macquarrie is not, *sensu stricto*, a process theologian, "he shares much in common with them."[22] Macquarrie's concept of Holy Being-letting-be achieves this degree of intimacy, this organic connection between God and the world.[23] The model of perfection that stands behind the monarchical concept of God is of an utterly transcendent and arelational God, an invulnerable God, sheerly impassible. Much modern Christian theology finds such a model of perfection deeply flawed, perhaps owing more to Greek philosophy than anything else. For many modern persons, process, relationality, vulnerability, and freedom are key and central aspects of perfection. Thus, David Tracy describes an alternative model of perfection:

> The relational, affecting, and affected person of modern process, Hegelian, and dialogical philosophies does provide more helpful candidates for possible models of human "perfection" than the ancient Greek models of the unaffected *(apatheia)* person (e.g., of the Stoics) or the modern liberal model of the purely autonomous individual. A relational model of human perfection is clearly a more adequate one for understanding divine perfection than either an ancient individualist or modern autonomous one.[24]

Macquarrie's seeing of God falls broadly within Tracy's sketch of an alternative model of perfection.

Needless to say, not all theologians share Macquarrie's *seeing* of the God-world relationship. Huw Parri Owen, writing out of a tradition of classical theism, finds Macquarrie's approach "both ontologically and logically illicit," and it is, given the ontological presuppositions of classical theism with which Owen was working.[25] Surely, the more foundational question remains: If two (or more) theistic systems are internally and logically free of fundamental contradiction, are coherent and cohesive, then the criteria for judging which is the more (or most) adequate must go beyond the purely logical into something like the *sanitas* or wholeness of which Allan Galloway speaks.

Macquarrie's understanding of God thus far is best understood as *panentheism,* "the belief that the Being of God includes and penetrates the whole universe, so that every part of it exists in him, but (as against pantheism) that this Being is more than, and is not exhausted by, the universe."[26] Although the term is somewhat cumbersome and Macquarrie himself tends to avoid its use, for purposes of brevity and exposition it serves its purpose. Panentheism seems to maintain balance between divine transcendence and immanence, always acknowledging the utter priority of God. It moves away from more infantile and severely anthropomorphic images of God, it invites a deep sense of perduring companionship with God, in whom everything lives and moves and has its being, and it looks forward in hope to the eschatological consummation of this companionship. Panentheism assists those who have struggled with images of God that no longer have the ability to hold together in harmony and challenge their ongoing multifaceted experience of reality in the modern world to reach a point of maturation in their spiritual and theological pilgrimage.

Marcus J. Borg, a New Testament scholar involved in the most recent quest of the historical Jesus, reveals how panentheism "made it possible for (him) to be a Christian again. The story of my own Christian and spiritual journey…involves the movement from supernatural theism through doubt and disbelief to panentheism. The God I have met as an adult is the God I never knew growing up in the church." As Borg explores panentheism in relation to Scripture and the Christian tradition, he acknowledges the work of John Macquarrie as having been particularly helpful.[27] Another popular theologian, sympathetic to panentheism yet critical of it, is the Anglican priest-physicist, John Polkinghorne, in his many books. He admits its achievement of balance between divine transcendence and immanence, but has difficulty with it in its process-theology proponents such as Charles Hartshorne, in whom it fails to accept the true otherness of the world from God, the classical doctrine of creation, the freedom of creation to be itself. While there is a family resemblance between Macquarrie and process theologians, he would share Polkinghorne's criticisms of the process version of panentheism. Macquarrie writes:

> I am not myself intending to make much use of the term "panentheism," though it must already be apparent that I have a good deal of sympathy with the position for which it stands....For my own part, I am content to call this position "dialectical theism," thereby stressing that it is essentially a species of theism and closer to theism than to pantheism, while the adjective "dialectical" makes it clear that I intend to avoid the one-sidedness of classical theism and the difficulties which it brought with it.[28]

It could be asserted that if what is described as "classical theism" had been more adequately understood and appropriated by its most eminent representatives, for example St. Thomas Aquinas, then the desired balance between transcendence and immanence would have been achieved without resort to "panentheism," although Macquarrie himself would question this claim: "Within the total framework of St. Thomas' classical theism, the weight given to immanence is not great."[29] Whether Macquarrie's judgment about St. Thomas is accurate or not is a very large question, but it seems to me that the fact remains that many people schooled and catechized in the classical tradition have not found it to be the case and reach out to something like panentheism as a conceptual tool that moves beyond what was seen as an absolute dualism between God and reality and best enables the integration of their religious experience. If we move beyond the understanding centrally expressed in *Principles of Christian Theology* to *In Search of Deity*, we may detect a further glossing of his panentheism in the direction of dialectical theism.

Dialectical Theism

In chapter 13 of *In Search of Deity* Macquarrie sets out the parameters of his "Dialectical Concept of God." In this book is to be found his most mature thinking about God, as he moves away from classical theism and moves beyond panentheism, a term that he finally finds "confusing and not particularly helpful."[30] However, as he proceeds to describe "dialectical theism," he recognizes the limitations of the exercise. He presents a series of dialectical oppositions within God, but with great care: "So far as possible, I must show that in every opposition, each side has its right and each side can and must be asserted. But I draw attention to the modifying expression, 'so far as possible,' for there must be limitations to any finite being's understanding of God. A 'God' understood and neatly packaged in philosophical concepts would not be God." There are six dialectical oppositions which "in their mutual tension…correct the deficiencies of each affirmation taken on its own."[31]

The first dialectical opposition is between being and nothing. Acknowledging the complexity of the language of being and its distinguished position as applied to God in the Christian tradition is his starting point. But obviously, as already noted, God does not exist in quite the same way as other entities. God is "not an item within the world." Hence, one may say that God is nothing, that is, no-thing. This way of speaking is an attempt to emphasize that God is the source of existence, the One who lets be all that is.

The second dialectical opposition is between the one and the many. As one it may be said that "God is the unity holding all things together and without which there would be chaos." At the same time, this oneness of God is not "a barren undifferentiated unity." Macquarrie believes that there is an inner differentiation in God that follows from understanding God as Being. There is the *primordial* mode of God's being, the ineffable-incomprehensible superexistence which lets-be everything that is. There is the *expressive* mode of God's being, the eternal event of giving in and through which God has shared existence with others. There is the *unitive* mode of God's being, whereby the cosmos seeks to return to its source in a deeper and richer unity. One is reminded here of an aphorism of Hans Urs von Balthasar, expressing the deep intimacy between God and creation:

> We belong more to God than to ourselves; thus, we are also more in him than in ourselves. Ours is only the way leading to the eternal image of us that he bears within himself. This way is like a carpet rolled out from him to us, a scroll *prodiens ex ore Altissimi*—"coming forth from the mouth of the Most High"—and we should, like children, learn how to copy it, how to trace the pre-scribed, pre-written characters that have been presented to us. The pre-scription, the law, is what Love has written out in advance, what Love presupposes and proposes to us that we might…become it.[32]

Balthasar is affirming the close connection between God's being and our being, a connection understood as a going forth from God and a return to God. In quite different language, that seems to be exactly what Macquarrie is talking about. Although there is an obvious trinitarian pattern in Macquarrie's language here, one notices that he has made no appeal to the data of Christian revelation. Rather, he is suggesting that "the doctrine of a triune God belongs to natural theology," and in earlier chapters of the book he has discerned this trinitarian pattern in such philosophical figures as Plotinus, Dionysius, Eriugena, Cusanus, Leibniz, Hegel, and Heidegger.

The third dialectical opposition is between God's knowability and his incomprehensibility. If God is expressive and unitive Being and not exclusively primordial Being, "then he does not confront us as a pure unknown." Knowledge of God is reached in the world "as a presence or as its unity," but such knowledge can never be exhaustive.

The fourth dialectical opposition is between God's transcendence and immanence. Macquarrie prefers a dynamic sense of transcendence "as God's capacity to go out from and beyond himself," that is to say, God's transcendence is supremely his capacity to let-be.

This is not to insist that creation is intrinsically necessary to God. It is to claim that God's very nature is to create, "to overflow himself in his generous bestowal of the gift of existence." Perhaps one might come close to Macquarrie's nuanced understanding here if one were to say that God had *almost* no choice but to create. On the other hand, God's immanence "refers to his indwelling of the creation, his presence and agency within the things and events of the world." In his judgment, classical theism emphasized the divine transcendence, the divine ontological otherness at the expense of the divine immanence. A favorite analogy of Macquarrie's for expressing God's immanent presence in creation is the analogy of the artist to his or her work. The analogy for him appears to originate in William Temple's Gifford Lectures, *Nature, Man and God*.[33] An artist puts something of himself into his work, so that to encounter the work is to encounter in a real sense the artist's presence. Macquarrie considers a hierarchy of truths expressive of God's immanent presence. First is the doctrine of creation itself, in which the goodness of matter is affirmed. Second is the doctrine of divine immanence within that creation. Third, in the emergence of human beings the divine presence reaches a new level of expression, with humankind created in the divine image. Finally, the incarnation of the Son, of expressive Being in Jesus of Nazareth, brings the expression of immanence to completion "so far." The process remains incomplete until the Parousia.

The fifth dialectical opposition is between impassibility and passibility. In classical theism God is pure act, and while God can affect creation, creation cannot affect God. God is impassible. Given Macquarrie's understanding of God's immanent presence within creation, "then he must be deeply affected by everything that goes on in the world...the suffering of that world must in some way be also experienced by God." Says Macquarrie,

I would not be able to subscribe to the impassibility of God. God must be the most sensitive reality that there is. If we could say that there is a kind of hierarchy of suffering as one moves up the chain

of being, then in some sense God must be the one who suffers most sensitively. I am aware of the patristic debate about whether God suffered, and so forth. But the Son could not have suffered without the Father suffering. I can't really think of God the Father as untouched by the suffering of the Son.

However, he recognizes that if we acknowledge that God suffers without nuance or gloss then God becomes nothing more than "a puny godling…the hapless victim of a world that has got completely out of control." God's passibility is then united to God's impassibility. God's suffering is different from the suffering of creatures. Macquarrie puts it like this:

> Whereas the suffering of a human being can overwhelm and eventually destroy the person concerned, this cannot happen in the case of God. He can accept the world's pain, and does in fact accept it because he is immanent in the world process, but he is never overwhelmed by it. He has an infinite capacity for absorbing suffering, and even for transforming it, though we cannot know how this transformation takes place.[34]

His argument for God's passibility is not left only at the level of the divine, as it were, in classical theism. It emerges also out of his own experience.

I had a colleague at Union Theological Seminary, Daniel Day Williams. I was a great admirer of Williams. After I left Union the school went through terrible troubles. Students were rebelling against the faculty, the faculty were divided among themselves, and in that situation Dan was a great reconciler, trying to heal these wounds. When I returned to Union for a visit, Dan asked me, "How long have you been away from Union?" "Three years," I replied. "Well," said he, "you chose three good years to be away." Within six months of that conversation he died of a heart attack. When I reflected on that, I couldn't help thinking "Dan has been so grieved by what was going on, and he has been taking into himself so much of the anger and pain." And it was then I thought that Dan was a godlike man. God takes the anger and pain of the world into himself and, because he is God, can transmute it. I would find it very hard to accept that God remains God regardless. You could think of God in his infinity as not only able but ready to embrace the suffering of the world and to absorb it into his own being. If I'm preaching or ministering to a sick person, I must be absolutely honest. I remember as a young minister being in a parish in Brechin for only a few weeks and the father of a young family was hospitalized with an incurable and inoperable cancer. And almost simultaneously his wife was taken to hospital with a tumour in the brain. What really hit me was when one of the orderlies from the hospital was passing me on his bicycle and he said, "I'm on my way up the hospital. Have you any message for Bruce?" I could not have felt more inadequate than at that moment. The answer, of course, is the Lord, the Word of God. Nowadays the first thing I'd do is take him holy communion. I'm not sure that classical metaphysical theism and Holy Scripture are entirely reconcilable on this point. A text that always impressed me from Isaiah is, "In all their afflictions he was afflicted." And a book I find very helpful in this regard is Moltmann's The Crucified God. *I regard it as one of the classics in theology of the twentieth century. I'm not sure that I accept all he has to say about Christ being rejected by God.*

His many comments on the suffering of God establish how important this topic is to Macquarrie.

Before leaving this dialectical opposition between passibility and impassibility, it is important to point out that many contemporary religious thinkers experience the need to develop an approach to God that reflects passibility in some degree. One thinks, for example, of Jurgen Moltmann, David Tracy, Paul S. Fiddes, Daniel Day Williams, about whom Macquarrie spoke so movingly, to name but a few representing different ecclesial traditions. Even a Thomist philosopher like W. Norris Clarke feels the need to revise his understanding of God. Clarke thinks that today we must speak of God as having a real relation to the world, requiring some qualification of God's immutability, including his impassibility.[35]

Finally, God is both eternal and temporal. If God is both passible and impassible, he has to be both temporal and eternal. Somehow, God is involved in the events of time, temporality, but is also immune from the ravages of time.

If one comes from a strictly Thomist standpoint, perhaps the clearest example of classical theism, then Macquarrie's dialectical theism will be found wanting. The English Dominican philosopher of religion Brian Davies, an established Thomist scholar, finds Macquarrie's dialectical theism disappointing and very close to the dipolar theism of process thinkers such as Whitehead and Hartshorne. For Davies, Macquarrie's real failure is to preserve the distinction between Creator and creation. A doctrine of creation ex nihilo, out of nothing, means quite simply that God is not a creature and cannot, therefore, be marked by any of the creaturely characteristics such as passibility.[36] This takes us really to the heart of the matter. If we operate with the principles of Thomist metaphysics as given, as axiomatic, then we have to rule out a priori Macquarrie's dialectical theism as unacceptable. If, however, that is not so and allowance is made for various metaphysical systems, including an alternative model of perfection, then within the framework of the metaphysics of dialectical theism, Macquarrie's vision seems most acceptable. Moreover, if it yields *sanitas,* health and balance, then it stands as a viable theology within the pluralism of Christian theologies.

The Theology of the Trinity

The doctrine of the Trinity is the Christian doctrine of God. Any doctrine or expression that is not trinitarian in character is not fully Christian. It is not the case that Christians have a basic belief in God which is common to other theists and then they add on to this basic concept further trinitarian specifications, as it were. The unipersonal God is not the Christian God. Cardinal Walter Kasper goes so far as to describe this unipersonal God as heresy: "From the theological standpoint we must speak more accurately of the heresy of theism. This theism with its unipersonal God is untenable...."[37] The doctrine of the Trinity is the "summary grammar" of the Christian account of God.

Nicholas Lash offers as a possible example of this heresy of theism a reference in the work of the Christian philosopher of religion, Richard Swinburne.[38] Swinburne defines a theist as "...[one] who believes that there is a God." So far so good, but then God is described as like "a person without a body (i.e., a spirit) who is eternal, free, able to do anything, knows everything, is perfectly good, is the proper object of human worship and obedience, the creator and sustainer of the universe." There are indeed elements in this description with which one would wish to be associated, that is, that God is eternal, free, perfectly good, the creator and sustainer of the universe. Unfortunately, this description lacks as a central aspect of Christian theism anything that is essentially trinitarian. It is almost as if the doctrine of the Trinity is a matter of believing some additional things about God beyond this agreed central core. This is not to impugn Swinburne's personal commitment as a Christian but to suggest that something absolutely fundamental is missing from this Christian description of God.

Traditional trinitarian language speaks of God as "one substance" and "three persons." Macquarrie thinks, like Karl Rahner and other theologians, that the word *person* has become unhelpful in articulating trinitarian convictions: "The word 'persons' has become so misleading that perhaps we would do better to think of 'movements' of Being, or 'modes' of Being (provided it is not in the sense of temporary modes)...."[39] Macquarrie's language may sound surprising, and perhaps even shocking to one who has a sense of the history of Christian doctrine and the pitfalls of modalism. William J. Hill, O.P., for example, describes Macquarrie's trinitarian theology as "neomodalism."[40] Hill thinks that since for Macquarrie the language of Father, Son, and Holy Spirit "is only the rendering of (divine

Being in its absoluteness) in Christian language, the doctrine assumes the character of a neomodalism. Hill is doubtful if Macquarrie's language of primordial, expressive, and unitive modes explains *real* distinctions in God. The real issue at stake in Hill's criticism has to do with theological method. If a theological method is correlational, as Macquarrie's clearly is in his existential ontology, then the distinctiveness and the reality of the Christian revelation may seem to evaporate in a mere naming of what is already given. The method of existential-ontological analysis finds a correlation between human existence and the symbols/doctrines of Christian revelation and teaching. If that is what is behind Hill's criticism, then the ground should shift to a more wide-ranging analysis of method in theology, and especially how one judges a given methodology to be adequate. However, this much at least may be said in support of Macquarrie's position, that it helps us to realize the inadequacy of all human language to speak God's reality. God is not a person, or three persons, in the same way that we are persons. In point of fact, Macquarrie is doing little more than St. Augustine when he affirmed that when we use the word *person* with regard to the Trinity, we mean by *person* whatever there are three of in the Trinity![41] If we think of *person* too literally, then we end up with tritheism, according to Macquarrie, and this is the reason why he regards the so-called social analogy for the Trinity as somewhat unsatisfactory. Those who advocate the social analogy think of *person* in the Trinity in relational terms, that is, that relationality is constitutive of personhood, that one person is no person, and they tend to distance themselves from the modern sense of *person* as a rational and autonomous subject. Macquarrie writes: "Even when we make every allowance for the fact that a person is constituted through his relation to other persons, such a model goes too far in the direction of 'dividing the substance'....But the social analogy has value in reminding us that because of the inescapable social dimension in man, any analogy between God and man must have in view man-in-community."[42] Despite Macquarrie's dislike of the social analogy for the reasons given, it seems virtually impossible to find a better word, a term that will express relationship between God and humankind. Perhaps the best that can be done in a sane (that is, related to *sanitas*) use of theological language is to use various models as mutually corrective in the common acknowledgement that all human language is ultimately inadequate in speaking of God.

God as Holy Being has let itself be known in the Christian community of faith under the trinitarian symbolism of Father, Son, and Holy Spirit. These three "persons" are not just three consecutive stages in the Christian community's experience or three temporal phases in God's self-manifestation, but rather belong to the very substance of the Godhead, Holy Being. Macquarrie proceeds to outline what he thinks of as his "dim conception" of the Blessed Trinity in terms that will be familiar from the consideration of his natural theology of the Trinity, in the consideration of his dialectical theism above.

"The Father may be called 'primordial' Being."[43] By this term he understands God the Father to be "the condition that there should be anything whatsoever, the source not only of whatever is but of all possibilities of being." The Father, as primordial Being, however, is never isolated, on his own, as it were. Rather, the very being of the Father is letting-be, "the source of outpouring" of being on others.

The Son may be called "expressive Being," because the energy of primordial Being "is poured out through expressive beings and gives rise to the world of particular beings....Being mediates itself to us through the beings." Although the description "expressive being" for the Son may seem strange, if we recall the wording of the Nicene Creed, we will see at once a similarity with Macquarrie's language for the Son. In the Creed, it is professed that "through [Christ] all things were made." Or, going earlier in the tradition to the Prologue of St. John's Gospel, we read "All things came to be through [the Word], and without him nothing came to be" (John 1.3). Macquarrie is giving philosophical expression, stemming ultimately from the categories of Martin Heidegger, to this biblical and credal conviction that through Jesus Christ, the Son, all reality has come to be. "The primordial being of the Father, which would otherwise be entirely hidden, flows out through expressive Being to find its expression in the world of beings."[44]

The Holy Spirit may be called "unitive Being," and this term is intended to recall the church's structure of prayer. The church generally ascribes glory to the Father and the Son "in the *unity* of the Holy Spirit." The Holy Spirit as unitive Being maintains, strengthens, and where necessary restores the unity of the beings with Being. The action of the Holy Spirit is a unifying action because it relates the beings to Holy Being. Wherever beings are seen not as self-subsistent, but as part of an integrated and larger whole, wherever unity is sought and maintained among all the entities that form God's good creation, there unitive Being, the Holy Spirit, is at work.

Elizabeth Johnson provides a fine summary of Macquarrie's trinitarian vision:

> In existential-ontological terms John Macquarrie works out the notion of Being as the energy of letting-be and self-spending. God who is Being itself is constituted by three persons, which are movements within the mystery of Being: primordial Being, deep overflowing source of all; expressive Being, mediating the dynamism outward; unitive Being, closing the circle to accomplish a rich unity in love.[45]

In some ways Johnson's expression in this summary improves upon Macquarrie's own expression, and provides a gloss on the remarks of Balthasar cited above about reality emerging from God and returning to God. God is the source of everything and the rich and fulfilling term of everything.

Not everyone will favor Macquarrie's "dim conception" (his own description) of the Trinity. Some will find this talk about Holy Being as primordial, expressive, and unitive obscure and unhelpful. Macquarrie's response would be to insist that there is no unclear, unambiguous language for God. God is Other, and the only language we can use to talk about the Other is faulty and frail human language. He finds that this kind of language is both helpful and credible in articulating the Christian doctrine of God, but he would insist that all responsible Christian forms of God-talk act as mutual correctives, pointing up the deficiencies in all God-talk. It seems to me, however, that the singular advantage behind Macquarrie's trinitarian language is that we as human beings get caught up in it. We are beings, individual beings, and therefore, have come to be through expressive Being, the Son. And, as Christians, that which maintains us in unity/union/communion with the primordial Being of the Father and the expressive being of the Son is unitive Being, the Holy Spirit. The doctrine of the Trinity in Macquarrie's form of expression is not extrinsic to us.

CHAPTER 3

Knowing Jesus Christ

Introduction

In my recent book on Christology I included a chapter, "How do we know Jesus Christ?" I tried to say there that you've got to introduce other ways of knowing besides the rational. You don't know Jesus Christ, even if you have read John Meier's books on the historical Jesus, as Meier himself really acknowledges. That's why my final chapter is actually called "The Metaphysical Christ." I'm not sure that it was a terribly good title for it, but it's Christ as the ultimate. There is also something about this in my book In Search of Humanity, *the chapter on cognition. Professor Gordon Stewart, professor of public health at Glasgow University, read* In Search of Humanity, *and he said the chapter he liked best was the one on cognition. To get a sense of what knowing besides the rational might mean, I like to quote St. Bonaventure: "First, therefore, I invite the reader to the groans of prayer through Christ crucified...so that he does not believe that reading is sufficient without unction, speculation without devotion, investigation without wonder, observation without joy, work without piety, knowledge without love, understanding without humility, endeavor without divine grace, reflection as a mirror without divine wisdom."*

The best place to look for an up-to-date précis of Macquarrie's Christology is undoubtedly his Cardinal Meyer Memorial Lectures at Mundelein Seminary, the Archdiocese of Chicago, in 1998. The lectures are published as *Christology Revisited*.[1] In a perceptive but not uncritical review the Cambridge theologian Lionel Wickham has captured Macquarrie's Christological tone: "John Macquarrie is an old hand at measured exposition. The clear language and serene tone of voice are welcome as ever."[2]

He is quite clear in the "introduction" that his intention is to pay particular attention to the Christological issues and difficulties that have been felt since the Enlightenment. Obviously, it is possible to advocate a Christology marked by the exemplarity of its patristic matrix or some other period in the two millennia of Christian tradition. But the value of Macquarrie's starting point is that it is where we are, that is to say, for better or worse we are living in a world strongly influenced by the Enlightenment. He characterizes the period since the Enlightenment as "an unprecedented era of theological renewal and creativity."[3] People's questions and concerns about Jesus Christ are shaped by that tradition in many respects. To neglect it in favor of an earlier period in the tradition seems pastorally misguided. One might wish to take people to a richer appreciation of the pre-Enlightenment tradition of Christological reflection, but first one must begin where people in fact are.

So, while acknowledging that "the Christology worked out in patristic times attained a classic status, and is indeed still the norm today," Macquarrie is insistent upon the need to do Christology *for today*. More precisely, the need is to reflect upon "the fundamental paradox, that Jesus Christ is both human and divine."[4] Accepting this paradox as the faith of the church, every intellectual effort must be made to understand some of it without avoiding the paradox through taking a shortcut. Docetists take a shortcut through Christ's humanity, adoptionists through his divinity. Both avoid what needs to be done: "We have rather to stretch our minds as far as they will go to show that this is indeed a paradox and by no means nonsense or mere contradiction."[5]

Starting from below, the humanity of Jesus is fully affirmed, with reference to the texts of the New Testament. There are many unequivocal testimonies to his humanity: He is tempted by Satan, he prayed to the Father, he was baptized by John, he experiences deep human emotions. Nonetheless, "from the very beginning or very near it, the disciples were discovering that there is something 'more' in Jesus that distinguishes him from the rest of the human race."[6] The Scottish Presbyterian theologian John McIntyre, a distinguished contributor to Christology with his *The Shape of Christology,* has well described Macquarrie's "something more" as "transcendental characteristics beyond the human…cognized by spiritual discernment, or quite simply faith."[7] That something "more" is engaged in five issues: the virginal conception, the miracles, the knowledge of Jesus, the sinlessness of Jesus, and the resurrection of Jesus. The difficulty, as Macquarrie sees it, is that these issues have often been understood in such a fashion that they appear to compromise Jesus' full humanity, and so he seeks an understanding of them that will not fatally compromise that humanity.

The Something More

First, the virginal conception. The standard issues are raised, that Paul and Mark know nothing of it, and that the account of it in Matthew is somewhat different from the account in Luke. Eschewing a purely biological approach, Macquarrie fixes on a theological interpretation as primary: "[Matthew and Luke] were saying that the life that had been implanted in Mary had come from God. Jesus Christ is not simply the product of natural evolution nor even of human procreation—there is something 'more' in Jesus…."[8] For the Gospel of St. John that something more is that Jesus comes from God, and Macquarrie points to the words from the Prologue found in John 1.12–13: "But to all who received him, he gave power to become children of God; who were born, not of blood nor of the will of the flesh nor of the will of man, but of God." While the latter part of the verse sounds as though it might be referring to a virginal conception/birth, in fact the words are applied to those who actually received him, to his followers. Macquarrie summarizes this point as follows: "Here the theological interpretation of the virgin birth is extended to those who have believed in Jesus. The individual Jesus is surrounded by a community that he has called into being, and together they constitute a new humanity, a new creation deriving from a new Adam, Jesus Christ, who realizes the intention of God where the old Adam had failed."[9] If the virgin birth is interpreted in this fashion, then for Macquarrie it does not infringe the full humanity of Christ. The value of the position is the ontological link that is clearly established between Jesus and the church, Christology and ecclesiology, a traditional affirmation of the broad Catholic tradition. Nonetheless, the question of the historicity of the virginal conception of Jesus, that is, the biological sense, remains an issue. In his book on Mary he adumbrates the theological interpretation given here, but in his *Jesus Christ in Modern Thought* he appears not to accept the historicity of the virgin birth.[10] When asked about this in the taped interview of July 1998, Macquarrie said that he remained agnostic about this issue.

The Miracles of Jesus

Second, the miracles of Jesus. If all the miracles attributed to Jesus in the Gospel narratives are accepted at face value historically, does this not mean that we have another version of docetism? Is this not an image of Christ as a supernatural being sweeping across the stage of history, and does this not infringe his true humanity and in fact render him incredible to modern people? Macquarrie has no difficulty acknowledging that Jesus healed people, though this ought not to be understood as a demonstration of divinity nor as an unqualified intrusion of divine power. He concludes:

> The relations of body and mind are still not understood, though they are obviously relations of a most intimate kind. Perhaps such healings will be much better understood in the future, but neither then nor now does it seem necessary to suppose that the agent or instrument of such healings

possesses magical or supernatural powers, though the gift which he or she exercises comes ultimately from God.[11]

Some will read Macquarrie here to be denying divine agency in miracle. However, the underlying issue is what model of divine agency is being presupposed. What is the relation between God and creation? Now Macquarrie's understanding of the relation is dialectical, or panentheistic, as we have seen in the last chapter, so that God is never absent from his creation, but may be understood as present with varying degrees of intensity, in given persons or places. Healings emerge when the intensity of the divine presence manifests itself in a particular context, in particular circumstances. What he wishes to avoid is an invasive sense of divine presence, and so of divine agency. If healing happens, then that is God's gift, whoever the instrument of that healing. He judges that "there are good reasons for doubting whether any nature miracles were ever performed by Jesus." His doubt is not merely symptomatic of the skeptical temper of the modern age, "but because Jesus himself rejected such actions and because they are incompatible with his true humanity." The refusal of Jesus in the temptation narratives (Matt 4.5–7, Luke 4.9–12) to impress the people through the performance of spectacular deeds is noted, as well as the docetist implications of the nature miracles. He offers two examples of a nondocetic interpretation of the nature miracles, Jesus walking on the Sea of Galilee, and the feeding of the multitude (especially in John 6). Walking on water, far from being a description of his supernatural, divine power is rather "a perfect description of the human condition." For Macquarrie the term conjures up all the insecurities and invulnerabilities of this life, and demonstrates Jesus' full humanity. The stories of feeding the multitudes are essentially to be understood as eucharistic allegories.

The Knowledge and Sinlessness of Jesus

The same mode of interpretation is followed through with regard to the knowledge of Jesus. He would not align himself with

Bultmann and others who judge the predictions of Jesus' passion to be *vaticinia ex eventu*—"that is perhaps going too far."[12] Jesus, with ordinary human knowledge, would have known the risks he was taking and what the possible/probable outcome could have been. But a detailed knowledge of the future and of his final denouement would not have been his.

What about Jesus' sinlessness? The Letter to the Hebrews affirms the sinlessness of Jesus in these words: "We have not a high priest who is unable to sympathize with our weaknesses, but one who in every respect has been tempted as we are, yet without sin" (Heb 4.15). This does not detract one iota from Jesus' humanity for Macquarrie because "sin is not part of human nature but a violation of human nature."

In all of this Macquarrie is aware of the response that suggests that this is to reduce Jesus to the merely human. He dislikes the phrase "merely human" because humanity has a marvelous destiny that is not captured in that description. Human beings are made in God's own image and likeness, and so to describe them as "merely human" is insufficiently appreciative of this dimension. Furthermore, to claim that Jesus is fully human is not necessarily to affirm that he is *only* human. "His humanity is not abolished by the presence of God in him but is transfigured into a true humanity. For the first time we are shown what the potentiality of humanity really is."

The Resurrection of Jesus

There has been no major development in Macquarrie's thinking on the resurrection of Christ since his *Principles of Christian Theology*. Even his *Jesus Christ in Modern Thought* does not carry a very extensive treatment of the resurrection.

For the writers of the New Testament the resurrection is always the work of God, the work of the Father, who raised up Christ from the dead. The resurrection thus tells us something about God, that his working never comes to a dead end, for he can always open up "a new possibility."[13] The resurrection reveals God, showing that his creative act is not limited, not even by the apparent impasse of death.

For Macquarrie, resurrection is not so much a clearly defined concept as a symbol or image "pointing to something which lies at the very limits of our understanding."[14] There are two basic ways of trying to understand and evaluate belief in the resurrection of Jesus: to begin with the reports of the New Testament or to begin from our present human experience.

The biblical accounts of the resurrection of Jesus are of two kinds: the empty-tomb stories and the stories of Jesus' appearances to his followers. Although there are certain discrepancies in the Gospel accounts of the discovery of the empty tomb, they all agree that certain women went to the tomb of Jesus to anoint his body but found the tomb empty. Similarly, there is disagreement among the witnesses about the details of Jesus' postresurrection appearances, but they are unanimous in insisting that some of Jesus' followers, both as individuals and in groups, experienced visions of Jesus, which they understood to mean he was alive.

With respect to the veracity of the empty-tomb stories, Macquarrie insists that Jesus' disciples were not in any way expecting his resurrection, so that there is little substance in the explanation "either that they had contrived the empty tomb or that they jumped to the conclusion that Jesus must have risen from the dead because his tomb was found empty."[15] He cites with approval the judgment of his Oxford colleague and authority on Second Temple Judaism, Geza Vermes: "When every argument has been considered and weighed, the only conclusion acceptable to the historian must be that the opinions of the orthodox, the liberal sympathizer and the critical agnostic alike—and even perhaps of the disciples them-selves—are simply interpretations of one disconcerting fact: namely, that the women who set out to pay their last respects to Jesus found, to their consternation, not a body, but an empty tomb." However, while the empty-tomb tradition must be taken seriously, "there is no straightforward route from the empirical fact of an empty tomb to the raising of the dead by God."[16]

Just as the empty-tomb stories are susceptible of various natural interpretations (e.g., secret removal of the body, going to the wrong tomb), so the reports of the appearances may be thought of in terms of psychological explanations (e.g., individual or mass hallucinations). The major negative factor in this type of naturalistic, psychological explanation—as in the case of the empty-tomb tradition—is the fact, upon which there is general scholarly agreement, that the disciples of Jesus were not expecting his resurrection, and so there was no motive force present as the ground for hallucination in the postresurrection appearances. There is one other point that militates against an hallucination theory, and that is the existence of the church. Macquarrie observes that "It is hard to believe that a community founded on hallucination could have survived for long, let alone have shown the unparalleled creative power of the Christian people of God."[17]

The historical fact of the church has to be taken into account in any serious discussion of the resurrection. No one disputes that the Christian community is and was a historical fact capable of verification. Yet, the fact that there is a church at all is dependent upon the transforming event or experience of the resurrection of Jesus.

Macquarrie asserts the continuity between the earliest Christians' experience and contemporary Christian experience, drawing upon the principle of analogy as it has been developed by Ernst Troeltsch: "The principle states that the report of an event will be more or less probable to the extent that we can point to analogous events in present experience."[18] In other words, it is only on the analogy of our own experience that historical understanding is possible at all. Gerald O'Collins implicitly accuses Macquarrie of affirming "a democracy of experience vis-à-vis the risen Christ."[19] However, O'Collins has not come to terms with the necessary epistemological base for affirming any historical judgment, that is, some fundamental continuity in our contemporary experience with the recorded experience of the past. There is no denial by Macquarrie of the recognition of the ontological novelty of the resurrection and, therefore, of the disciples' experience of this in the Scriptures. But the

Christ experienced in Christian liturgy and witness today cannot be a different Christ. As Macquarrie puts it, "The report of a resurrection would be very difficult to accept unless we could point to some present experience."[20]

Noting the hazards of speculation about the resurrection, Macquarrie thinks that in 1 Corinthians 15 St. Paul provides "a substantial piece of theological reflection" on the resurrection. The resurrection is not the reanimation of a corpse, but has to do with a "spiritual body" (1 Cor 15.44). Macquarrie interprets this as meaning "a new mode of existence in which the person is incorporated into the life of God." For Paul, this new mode of existence is every man's destiny, though Jesus Christ is the first to attain it. Jesus in the resurrection remains alive, and not just in and with his community, but with God, "no longer bounded with the particularities of a human existence in space and time."[21] Jesus has fulfilled the potentialities of human existence and indeed raised that existence to a new level; he has revealed its potentiality for an eternal life in God; he has "abolished death and brought life and immortality to light" (2 Tim 1.10).

What is meant by this fulfillment of the potentialities of human existence? It means essentially that Christ has brought to light a true humanity, showing what human beings have it in them to become. In Jesus we see the qualities that are essential to a true humanity, such qualities as love, freedom, integrity, creativity, moral sensitivity, and resurrection, because resurrection has as "an important part of its meaning, precisely the emergence of a new level of human and personal existence."[22] This new level of human and personal existence will elude our understanding so long as "we are seeing it only from below." If Jesus is the fulfillment of the potentialities of human existence, the resurrection is necessarily part of this fulfillment, because in the resurrection "he now lives as one sharing in the eternal life of God."[23]

Adoptionism

In stressing, or in attempting to give due weight to the humanity of Jesus, there often lurks in the background the suspicion that one might be an adoptionist in respect of his divinity. *Adoptionism* is something of a slippery term, but Macquarrie provides a broad definition of it: "the type of Christological theory which, it is usually believed, so emphasizes the humanity of Christ that it rules out any special ontological or metaphysical relation between him and the Father."[24] He notes further that the term gets used rather loosely today to describe those theologians who may criticize some or other elements of the Christology consequent upon the Council of Chalcedon (451) that have so shaped the Christian tradition.

A key, if not the key issue in adoptionism is the pre-existence of Jesus Christ. Did Jesus Christ qua Jesus Christ pre-exist his incarnation in the womb of Mary? Macquarrie had articulated his position as early as 1966 in an article entitled "The Pre-Existence of Jesus Christ." In that article he had said:

> The idea of pre-existence, like so many other ideas in the New Testament, does have a value that lies obscured beneath its mythological associations, and that it would be wrong to reject pre-existence in favour of a thorough going adoptionism. Rather, we ought to look more closely at the idea of pre-existence, and see whether we can restate its essential meaning in a language that would be intelligible to our time.[25]

If pre-existence in the mind and purpose of God may be equated with real pre-existence, then Macquarrie has no particular difficulty with it. If the Logos is coeternal with the Father and if the Logos became flesh in our Lady's womb as Jesus of Nazareth, then some intelligibility can be made out of pre-existence. However, this seems different from a personal pre-existence, in some way an "embodied" pre-existence of Jesus Christ as such. In *Jesus Christ in Modern Thought* this is how he expresses himself:

> ...I have consistently argued that if there is some *nisus* or goal-seeking striving in the evolutionary process, it is better

understood in immanental terms than as imposed from outside by a transcendent "watchmaker." But I am saying that (however one may interpret the matter), this earth, the human race, yes, Jesus Christ himself were already latent, already predestined, in the primaeval swirling cloud of particles."[26]

There remains a fear that the language and expression of Macquarrie about pre-existence somehow detracts from the tradition of Christological orthodoxy. Perhaps this fear is founded on a failure to recognize that all language about Christ and God limps and no language is perfect. However, one may go further and ask about the function and role of the language of pre-existence. Gerald O'Collins, S.J. has suggested a possible way forward here. "Pre-existence means…that Christ personally belongs to an order of being other than the created, temporal one. His personal, divine existence transcends temporal (and spatial) categories; it might be better expressed as trans-existence, meta-existence, or, quite simply, eternal existence."[27] Furthermore, O'Collins takes Macquarrie to task in suggesting that "he fails to see that personal pre-existence does not mean that Jesus eternally pre-existed *qua Jesus*. His humanity first came into existence as such around 5 B.C. The human consciousness of Jesus did not pre-exist 'in heaven.'"[28]

Three criteria may be posited for distinguishing an incarnational Christology from various kinds of reductionist Christologies: The initiative comes from God; God is deeply and intimately involved in creation; the center of this initiative and involvement is Jesus Christ. If these three criteria may be shown to be present in a given Christology, then it may not be judged adoptionist or reductionist.

The three criteria fit his understanding of the incarnation: "…the unitary person, leading edge, or *hypostasis* of Jesus was not the *hypostasis* of the divine Logos displacing the human *hypostasis* and using the body of Jesus as a mere instrument, nor was it a composite *hypostasis* constituting Jesus a new species distinct from *homo sapiens,* but was the human *hypostasis* transfigured by a constant immersion in the divine Spirit." Jesus Christ, constantly immersed in the divine Spirit, is different from the rest of humanity in degree rather than in kind. A difference of degree "may be so great that for all practical purposes it counts as a difference of kind."[29] Returning to his *Jesus Christ in Modern Thought,* this is how he understands incarnation: "…it is the progressive presencing and self-manifestation of the Logos in the physical and historical world. For the Christian, this process reaches its climax in Jesus Christ, but the Christ-event is not isolated from the whole series of events. That is why we can say that the difference between Christ and other agents of the Logos is one of degree, not of kind."[30]

Christ and Other Faiths

If the difference between Christ and other agents of the Logos is one of degree and not of kind, then we are led into this difficult and complex issue of understanding the relationship between him and other savior figures of the world's religions. In an essay responding to Paul Knitter, a Catholic theologian whose work is marked by a strong interest in this matter of the uniqueness of Jesus Christ, Macquarrie outlines his understanding of that uniqueness. The gist of it is given in his own words:

> I have urged the case for a combination of "commitment" and "openness" on the part of the religious believer, that is to say, a full commitment to one's own faith and to its mediator (in my own case, this would be to Christianity and Jesus Christ), yet at the same time an "openness" towards other faiths and other mediators, in the sense of acknowledging that God has made himself known and has made salvation available through these other channels also.[31]

Starting with the New Testament, one can see that there are various Christologies, sometimes in tension with one another, even within the same book. For example, in the Acts of the Apostles 4.12 St. Peter preaches before the Jewish Sanhedrin that "There is no salvation through anyone else, nor is there any other name under heaven given to the human race by which we are to be saved." When we come to Acts 17 and St. Paul's speech to the Athenians, he appears to presuppose some common ground between Greek religiosity and himself. Turning to St. John's Gospel, the affirmation is found that "No one comes to the Father except through [Jesus]" (14.6), but at the same time the Logos "was the light of the human race," and the implication seems to be that this light somehow enlightens everyone (1.4). Finally, in the Letter to the Hebrews a unique priestly role is given to Jesus Christ, but within "a great cloud of witnesses" including Abel, Enoch, and Noah, as well as Abraham and Moses (Heb 11). In summary, there appear to be both exclusive and inclusive Christologies in the New Testament, which perdure through the patristic period, and perhaps the inclusivist view "was never suppressed." Macquarrie comments on the basis of such texts and references that "from creation onward, God (or the Logos, if one prefers) has been incarnating itself in the world in many ways and in many degrees," and he cites (albeit without the precise reference) Teilhard de Chardin, "The prodigious expanses of time which preceded the first Christmas were not empty of Christ."[32] The incarnation is "the culminating point of what God has been doing in all history."[33] Macquarrie finds this approach exemplified in St. Athanasius: "The philosophers of the Greeks say the world is a great body; and rightly they say so, for we perceive it and its parts affecting our senses. If then the Word of God is in the world, which is a body, and he has passed into it all and into every part of it, what is wonderful or what is unfitting in our saying that he came in a man?"[34] It is of course one thing to say that God is immanent in the world, and something else entirely that he is equally immanent in everything. The latter would be a crude form of pantheism. The former provides Macquarrie with a way of maintaining the climactic expression of the divine immanence in the incarnation of Jesus Christ, "in whom God was signally present," but without denying other expressions of the divine immanence, or degrees of incarnation in other savior figures. If in fact the point of religion is to achieve union between the divine and the human, something like "incarnation" seems required: "...incarnation would seem to instantiate such a union in the most intimate way conceivable."[35] Thus, if incarnation is not associated exclusively and uniquely with Jesus Christ, it may not be an insuperable barrier to dialogue among the religions.

Given this approach, dialogue among the religions becomes a moral imperative. This does not make mission or proclamation redundant for Macquarrie. He maintains that "There probably is still a place for the old-fashioned type of missionary proclamation, especially in the secularized nations of Europe and North America." However, dialogue does not go far enough for him. Using the example of the late Mother Teresa of Calcutta, he suggests that service of others, while not taking the place of dialogue, speaks a more profound missionary message.

Christ is definitive for the Christian not only of the nature of God, but also of the nature of the human person. There cannot be "a *full* revelation of God, for the infinite cannot be fully comprehended in the finite" and this same acknowledgment of finitude "prevents us from embracing an unlimited pluralism."[36] It would be exceedingly difficult if not impossible for a person to become genuinely conversant with and fluent in other faiths, even one other faith. From the vantage point of the ordinary human being, the choice would seem to be between deepening one's own faith or becoming a dilettante. To maintain that Christianity is definitive for oneself, or for Christians, is a way of saying "that within my limited faith and experience, Jesus Christ is *sufficient*. Through him I think I have been brought into relation to God." A Christian, therefore, is committed to Jesus Christ, but at the same time is open to the truths to be found in other faiths.

Knowing Jesus Christ

Central to any and all discussion of Christology is what constitutes "knowing Jesus Christ." Or, what constitutes knowledge? There are different ways of knowing, according to Macquarrie. If we turn to the chapter entitled "Cognition" in his *In Search of Humanity,* the chapter that the Glasgow surgeon Gordon Stewart (mentioned earlier) found so attractive, then we find the lineaments of Macquarrie's epistemology. In this chapter he discusses the theories of Karl Popper and Michael Polanyi to break open the widespread, commonsense empiricism that characterizes so much of the Western world. He sees Popper and Polanyi as "a pincer movement threatening the core of conventional empiricism," and he proceeds to list seven principles that inform his work.[37]

1. *That some knowledge does not begin from observation.*
2. *That conjectures and imaginative hypotheses (even, and perhaps especially, improbable ones!) may be more fruitful than inductive generalizations.*
3. *That in many subjects, and not least in the study of humanity itself, the ideal of detachment is a hindrance.*
4. *That knowledge is a function of an active self participating in a world rather than the data collected by an abstract thinking subject.*
5. *That there are various kinds of tacit knowledge, ranging all the way from the skills of craftsmen to the insights of artists and even the visions of mystics, and these cannot be put into propositions expressed in clear and distinct ideas.*
6. *That knowledge of facts expressed in propositions is one kind of knowledge among others and has to be considered in the context of more direct forms of knowledge by participation, including knowledge of things, knowledge of other people, and knowledge of ourselves.*
7. *That finally the concept of knowledge is far broader and richer than the narrower type of empiricist epistemology is prepared to concede.*

Each of the statements could be defended, as Macquarrie in fact does, but the backdrop to them all is the permeative position of those who would claim that only objective empirical knowledge counts as real knowledge. This is hardly adequate when it comes to knowing art, another person, a spouse, or God. Nor does it get us very far in knowing Jesus Christ. Statements 5 and 6 are further articulated Christologically in his *Christology Revisited*. Accumulating historical knowledge/data about Jesus is clearly legitimate, but such information would lack any sense of encounter, confrontation, or engagement with him as anything more than a figure of the past. Macquarrie disallows too sharp a distinction between historical knowledge, the testimony of the past, and knowledge that comes through present experience. Christians do not come to knowledge of Christ simply from the reading of the Scriptures, as though they were reading of some great historical figure. Such a view would entirely fail to realize the connection between Christ and the church. "The church is the Body of Christ, continuing his presence on earth. To quote Michael Ramsey, 'The fact of Christ includes the fact of the Church.'"[38] This fact yields a knowledge of Christ that is "spiritually discerned," but in no fashion arbitrary. It is like "seeing in depth," seeing the inward constitutive meaning of things. For that reason, he is also cautionary about a critical reading of the Gospels: "If we read the Gospels primarily in a critical way, we are not likely to be encountered by Christ in them." Such an excessively critical reading of the Gospels almost presupposes a model of knowledge that Macquarrie is trying to expand, the model of neutral, systematic, objective knowledge.

There is knowledge born of love. "Love could be described as a way of knowing.... All kinds of love have a cognitive component."[39] Using an example from ordinary human experience, he notes that one who "loves" his subject will notice and attend to things that someone who is indifferent might miss. The insight becomes enlarged when speaking of Christ. Here Macquarrie is approximating what can only be called the cognitive dimension of mysticism. In point of fact, he describes mystical knowing: "Perhaps the highest reach of faith is found in mysticism, which I take to be a kind of total immersion in the divine and therefore perhaps the highest level of knowledge possible for a human being on earth."[40]

The Christ known in the knowledge of love, by that special "spiritual discernment" that is consequent upon love, the Christ of mysticism is also the "metaphysical Christ." Following Dietrich Bonhoeffer's *Christ at the Center,* Macquarrie finds three focal points about this Christ: Christ as the center of human existence, as the center of history, as the mediator between God and nature. In other words, if Christ is at the center, at the center of everything, then what is outside the circumference is quite literally *nothing.* The metaphysical Christ is the all-pervasive Christ, in whom we live and move and have our being, so that "reality' is Jesus Christ."[41]

Conclusion

In an interesting but tantalizingly brief comparison of the Christologies of Macquarrie and Hans Urs von Balthasar, Francesca Murphy seems to conclude that Balthasar's Christology "from above" is realist, stemming from a realist metaphysic, while Macquarrie's Christology "from below" is idealist, flowing from an idealist metaphysic.[42] Perhaps this in a sense gets us to the heart of the matter. Realism may be defined as a philosophical position affirming that reality exists independently of the human knowing subject, and idealism as a philosophical tradition originating with Plato which understands the mind, ideas, or spirit as fundamental and basic to reality. One must affirm that reality exists outside the knower, as it were. That seems to be plain common sense. At the same time, there can be no awareness of reality without the knowing subject. One may not be had without the other. If Macquarrie evinces a contemporary Platonic rendering of reality in terms of degrees of being, of Christology in terms of degrees of divine immanence, and if that rendering engages many people in a fashion that satisfies the curiosity of the theological mind, and in a way that satisfies the linguistic and regulative conventions of Christian orthodoxy, may one ask for more? In terms used earlier, if Macquarrie's theological metaphysics yields a *sanitas* both theologically from within the Christian tradition, and metaphysically, then it stands.

CHAPTER 4

Church and Sacrament

The Century of the Church

This century has been described by Otto Dibelius as the "century of the Church."[1] Behind this remark lies the ecumenical movement that got under way after the Edinburgh Missionary Conference in 1910, paving the way for the establishment of the World Council of Churches in Amsterdam in 1948. The renewal of ecclesiology in the Catholic Church is another factor in the making of this ecclesial century, a renewal fueled by Vatican Council II, especially its Constitution on the Church and Decree on Ecumenism. With the publication of these documents the Catholic Church moved into the ecumenical movement and has remained committed to it ever since. As Vatican II moved to its conclusion in 1965, John Macquarrie moved from the Presbyterianism in which he had been brought up and in which he had ministered to the Anglican Communion. This took place while he was teaching at Union Theological Seminary in New York. He had felt the attraction of the Episcopal Church, as the Anglican Communion is known in Scotland, from his youth, and he tells us that "Back in Scotland, and for family reasons, it was difficult for me to break away from the prevailing Presbyterianism and I had been a Presbyterian minister since 1944."[2] In 1965 he was ordained a priest in the Anglican Communion. During this New York period he had also readied his *Principles of Christian Theology,* in which he provides an account of his ecclesiology, an ecclesiology that obviously reflected his new ecclesial allegiance. In 1975 he followed this with *Christian Unity and Christian Diversity,* in which he treated of ecumenism and ecumenical theology. Using these books as our primary sources we shall present an account of Macquarrie's ecclesiology. The one thing that is immediately noticeable about Macquarrie's ecclesiology is that it does not indulge in "narcissism," an introversion of the church upon herself that can all too easily slide into place. Macquarrie has no time for that kind of ecclesiology. His ecclesiology describes a church that is connected with the world, that is not self-seeking, and that attempts to engage with difficult questions honestly.

The Church in Relation to Other Christian Doctrines

All of Christian doctrine is interconnected, so that to engage with one doctrine is inevitably to find oneself engaged with another, and ultimately with the entire fabric of Christian teaching. In this vein Macquarrie sees the church knit into other doctrines. First, the church must be understood in relation to the doctrine of creation. "The Church is already implicit in creation."[3] The church is there in the beginning, from the beginning. There has always been a community of faith in the world, "as far back as we can go," well captured in Hebrews 11.4–7. In that sense the entire human race constitutes the people of God, but "this does not detract from the need for a special group, a special people whose destiny and service it is to realize and to represent an authentic existence for all….[The church] is the spearhead of what is going on in the creation as a whole."[4]

Moving toward the doctrine of the incarnation, the church finds its most distinctive title as the "body of Christ" (1 Cor 12.27; Eph 1.23; Col 1.18). The church, those "in Christ," are being "conformed to Christhood," as they participate in the Paschal Mystery. The church is those who are re-created in Christ, so that it becomes in John Knox's words "the historical embodiment of the new humanity."[5] In this light one may speak of the church legitimately as the "extension" of the incarnation, though care must be taken not to mistake the church in its complete and final condition. "The incarnation which reached its completion in (Christ) is in process in the Church. Our hope is indeed that it is moving toward completion in the Church too, but at any given time, the Church is a mixed body. It is not free from sin, and there may even be times when it slips back."[6]

The doctrine of "the last things" comes next. The church is not to be identified with the Kingdom of God without qualification, but nor can it be simply distinguished from the kingdom. "We may think of the kingdom as the entelechy of the Church, the perfect unfolding of the potentialities that are already manifesting themselves in the Church."[7] The church is the anticipation of the kingdom, *the* sacrament of the kingdom.

The Marks of the Church

The four traditional marks of the church are unity, holiness, catholicity, and apostolicity. "The Christian hope is that these notes will come through more and more clearly as the Church moves towards its consummation."[8] The first note of the church is unity, the center of which is Jesus Christ himself. Since Christ is the head of the body, the church, he is the source of that body's unity. The unity of the body, however, is not to be identified with uniformity. Macquarrie underscores the insight of St. Paul that unity and diversity go together, as in that wonderful passage of 1 Corinthians 12. The challenge is to maintain unity and diversity in a fine balance, eschewing both uniformity and autonomy, and the key is the doctrine of the holy Trinity. In the Trinity the unity of God is expressed in the three persons of the Trinity: "The ultimate model for the Church's unity is therefore the unity of the triune God, a unity embracing the richest diversity and thus one in which there is neither stifling absorption nor damaging division."[9]

Perhaps we can see here an ecclesiology of communion in Macquarrie, communion being a central ecclesiological concept in contemporary theology. "Communion" clearly does not have the developed place in Macquarrie's ecclesiology that it enjoys in today's ecumenical reflection on the church. One thinks, for example, of the influential work of the Greek Orthodox theologian Metropolitan John D. Zizioulas and the Catholic Jean M. R. Tillard, O.P. In both of these authors communion is a key category for understanding the church.[10] This is missing in Macquarrie, at least as an explicit, ecumenical, ecclesiological, category. However, insofar as communion is seen to be ecclesial participation in the life of the Trinity—and one recognizes that it is more nuanced than this bald statement would lead to believe—then this is reflected in Macquarrie's thought.

The second note of the church is holiness. Holiness means "being an agent of the incarnation, letting Christ be formed in the Church and in the world."[11] This formation of Christ that is both ecclesial and cosmic in scope is always partial and unfulfilled before the Parousia. The church is always the church *in via,* on the way. It is a church in the pellucid phrase of Aidan Nichols, O.P., echoing an Augustinian emphasis, in which sinners "are hospitalized...with a view to being made well, and made saints."[12]

Catholicity is the third note of the church, and it includes two distinct but related ideas. First, is the notion of "universality." The church is for all people everywhere, transcending all cultures. "It is this inclusive unity-in-diversity that constitutes the catholicity of the church as universality."[13] Secondly, catholicity also means authenticity, "authenticity of belief and practice in the church." The authentic faith is learned from the church as a whole, from the universal church, and so this second sense of catholicity is related to the first. Councils of the church, expressive of the consensus of the faithful, is a primary measure of catholicity, for example, in giving rise to the creeds of Christianity, formulated under the guidance of the Holy Spirit. The catholicity of the church in this double sense preserves the church from the dangers of insularity and even ethnocentrism on the one hand, and from loss of identity on the other.

The final mark of the church is apostolicity. It consists in "the church's own living continuity with the apostles."[14] Macquarrie draws a helpful analogy for apostolicity with the development of the self: "As the commitment of faith plays an important part in unifying a self, so that we can recognize it as the same self as it moves through time, so too the community of faith is united by the same faith that has spanned the centuries. The formulations of that faith have changed and will change, but the existential attitude which constitutes the core of the faith, has remained constant."[15] The obvious question now is, "How is apostolicity maintained in practice?" The answer is for Macquarrie that the episcopate is the institutional form that protects apostolicity. "This office, publicly transmitted by the apostles to their successors and then on through the generations, is the overt, institutional vehicle for ensuring the continuity of that heritage of faith and practice which was likewise transmitted by the apostles."[16] Macquarrie finds himself in agreement with his Union Theological Seminary colleague, John Knox, when he says, "I for one have no hesitancy in ascribing the same status to episcopacy as to canon and creed."[17] Historically the church exhibits these four marks in a "more or less" fashion until it reaches its completion in the Kingdom of God.

The Petrine Ministry

Macquarrie's views of the Petrine Ministry have undergone considerable development over the course of his theological career. Writing an Anglican reply in 1970 to the question, "What Still Separates Us from the Catholic Church?" Macquarrie insists that the Anglican Communion does not consider itself separate from the Catholic Church: "Anglicanism has never considered itself to be a sect or denomination originating in the sixteenth century. It continues without a break the *Ecclesia Anglicana* founded by St. Augustine thirteen centuries and more ago, though nowadays that branch of the church has spread far beyond the borders of England." The question is better formulated in this way: "What still separates Anglicans and Romans *within* the Catholic Church to which they so visibly and manifestly belong?"[18] Responding to the question thus phrased, Macquarrie went on to give his attention to the papacy, and it has remained a published interest of his. "At the very least, we have to affirm that any vision of a reunited church, one, holy, catholic and apostolic, must envisage it in communion with the most illustrious of the apostolic sees. Anything short of this can be regarded only as an interim step; and anything that might make this ultimate consummation more difficult should be scrupulously avoided."[19] Thus does Macquarrie begin his first treatment of the papacy in his *Principles.*

The New Testament in his judgment makes clear the special status, the primacy of St. Peter among the apostles: his recognition of Jesus as Messiah (Mark 8.29); Christ's declaration that he was the rock on which he will build the church (Matt 16.18); he was the first of the apostles to see the risen Christ (1 Cor 15.5, etc.); and it is to Peter that the risen Christ commends the care of the church in the Gospel of John (John 21.15–19); in the Acts of the Apostles Peter acts as a spokesman for the church; Peter is the first to open the church to the Gentiles; even when Paul has a disagreement with Peter, he makes it abundantly clear that he acknowledges the special place Peter has in the church.[20] Though there are historical obscurities in the postapostolic church about the development of the Petrine ministry, Macquarrie does not see this as a significant problem. Rather, the same kind of obscurity obtains in respect of the rise of the New Testament canon, the development of the sacraments, and the emergence of the threefold shape of ministry (diaconate, presbyterate, episcopate). "If we are to call the latter three apostolic, should we deny the title to the papacy?"[21] Just as these have been instrumental in nurturing the unity and integrity if the church, so has the papacy.

The central problematic issue for Macquarrie is infallibility. He admits a basic meaning to the doctrine, a freedom from error, the quality of indefectibility: "For what is freedom from error if it is not penetration into truth? Could we say that just as a compass needle, when distracting influences have been removed, turns unfailingly toward the north, so the mind of the church, when fully open to the Holy Spirit, turns unfailingly toward the truth?"[22] Indefectibility, thus understood, is not infallibility. Indefectibility is for him an eschatological idea, "but when we talk of 'infallibility,' we are asking about the kind of guidance available to the church *in via*."[23] The doctrine of infallibility implies that "given certain carefully specified conditions...on a particular occasion and on a particular matter one can assert that the Pope (or the church) has made a pronouncement that is guaranteed to be free from error."

Writing in 1975, Macquarrie judged this doctrine to be such a formidable obstacle that "(he did) not see any way in which this doctrine could ever become acceptable to Anglicans and Protestants."[24] This description is in his own words "in very negative terms."[25] In his later essay, "The Papacy in a Unified Church," Macquarrie comes to a more positive judgment on infallibility, based on the insights of the late Bishop Christopher Butler, two insights in particular.[26] First, Butler maintained that any verbal expression is necessarily involved in the fallibilities of language, so that, as a result, it may be "inadequate, misleading, and even trailing clouds (of culturally derived error)." This allays some of Macquarrie's anxiety about any linguistic formula being utterly free of error. Butler emphasized that one ought to look at the governing intention behind the term. The actual term *infallibility* is a negative term, that is to say, "it seems to stress the negative notion of inerrancy, whereas what is really at stake is guaranteed truth—a positive notion." Macquarrie still has some difficulty with the expression "guaranteed truth," but recognizes behind it the pneumatological conviction that the Holy Spirit will lead the church into the fullness of truth, using his analogy of the magnetic needle. At the same time, he also accepts that this infallibility, a gift to the whole church, may be exercised in a special way by "the one who leads the church." This leadership, however, must be seen in a corporate or collegial context.[27] Understood in this fashion the dogma of papal infallibility may make sense to Christians not in full communion with Rome.

Invited to comment on Macquarrie's essay "The Papacy in a Unified Church," the Irish systematic theologian Eamonn Conway rightly suggests that the Catholic understanding of infallibility, though very close to his point of view, actually goes further than Macquarrie. He uses the analogy of the magnetic needle to good effect to establish his point: "...the doctrine of papal infallibility claims that, at *particular* decisive moments on its journey the Christian community can be assured that the compass needle is not under any distracting influences and is, in fact, pointing north."[28] But, having said that, Conway insists that, given the stricture that all human language is conditioned by circumstances, noted by Butler and accepted by Macquarrie, "even a defined doctrine is open to development not just in terms of its formulation but also in terms of its content."

The indefectible relation to truth pertains to the whole church and its leadership. In this way Macquarrie sees the role and function of the papacy within the episcopate, as having a primacy within the episcopate: "…a papacy truly integrated with the bishops and eventually with the whole people of God. The Pope is a sacramental person, an embodiment of the whole church, but he is nothing apart from the church."[29] This is Macquarrie's version of what Vatican Council II called "collegiality," a collegiality that he sees first expressed in the apostolic period: "…the scriptural record seems to visualize the leadership of Peter, but it is not a monarchical leadership, but one exercised in consultation with colleagues."[30]

Ecumenism

Consistently throughout his entire oeuvre Macquarrie insists on a legitimate pluralism in the church, provided that this pluralism does not lead to a basic lack of cohesion. Uniformity is not synonymous with unity.[31] He is, therefore, suspicious of a unity that would fail to acknowledge and respect the different Christian ecclesial traditions.

He sees a paradigm of a single Christian communion that combines both unity and pluralism exemplified in his own Anglican Communion. "Anglicans affirm the basic doctrines of Catholic faith, but allow latitude in the interpretation of these doctrines and believe that free but responsible theological discussion rather than appeal to a detailed *magisterium* is the best way of sifting truth from falsity."[32]

Because of this panoramic vision of a united Christian communion, but not uniform in expression, Macquarrie is utterly opposed to schemes of Christian union, schemes based on national or geographical lines particularly. The various Christian traditions have their own integrity and, "like an art style, cannot be mixed with other traditions without loss of its distinctive appeals."[33] He makes the cogent point that "In the history of religions, syncretism has always proved to be a weakness and there is no reason to suppose that it would be any different in the context of Christian ecumenism." For Macquarrie one of the most worrying concerns of the ecumenical movement is this failure to recognize the value of the various Christian traditions, and he is quite scathing in his criticism of a certain kind of ecumenist: "There has come into being a kind of ecclesiastical jet set, whose members seem always to be on the point of departing for conferences in Jakarta or Uppsala, or just getting back from other conferences in Accra or Caracas."[34] Most schemes of union for Macquarrie seem to aim at the greatest degree of compromise and uniformity. The best existing model for Christian unity, as he explores it in his 1975 *Christian Unity and Christian Diversity,* is the uniate model, "which we find in the relation of the Roman Catholic Church and the so-called 'Uniate' churches of the East." His concern is not with the way that these unions came about historically, "some of them decidedly shady." The value is in the model itself, which at the same time allows union with Rome and a measure of autonomy for the individual churches, for example, in the areas of liturgy and canon law. The uniate model thus keeps together both values of unity and legitimate pluralism.

His position has not been without its critics, most notably the late Lesslie Newbigin, bishop of the Church of South India, an ecumenically united church. Newbigin immediately points out that whether one likes it or not, united churches have proliferated and that "millions of Christians are living in such united churches, daily thanking God for the blessing of unity."[35] Newbigin, as a lifelong committed ecumenist, had a much clearer vision of the impact of such church unions than Macquarrie. His own experience in the united Church of South India bears witness to at least the value of that successful experiment in church union. Bishop Newbigin writes:

In 1965, after an absence of eighteen years, I returned to Madras as bishop to serve the same churches which I had known two decades earlier as competing congregations. I did not find that they had become uniform: on the contrary I found a rich variety of styles in worship and practice. What I found was congregations less concerned about their own affairs and more ready to think in terms of God's will for the life of the city as a whole, less like competing clubs each trying to enlarge itself and a little more recognizable as sign and foretaste of God's kingdom.[36]

Where church unions function in this way, the problems to which Macquarrie was drawing attention are diminished.

It is also difficult to avoid the conclusion that Macquarrie's antipathy toward pragmatic ecumenical solutions is much colored by the theology of his Glasgow doctoral supervisor, Ian Henderson. Henderson deeply distrusted what he took to be schemes of ecclesial union that neglected in principle the particularities of churches.

In (Henderson's) *Power Without Glory* the implied criticism of ecumenical theology is greatly developed. Here he makes the point that ecumenical language "is designed not to describe but to conceal" and that it is "a fiesta of double-think".…There is a language which conceals in order to evade, a language which does not explore open theological possibilities but rather manipulates the data in order to arrive at predetermined results.[37]

Macquarrie does not share every aspect of Henderson's point of view as is established in his personal and published commitment to ecumenism, but there remains a lingering distrust of pragmatic bureaucracy that can seem to give short shrift to important theological presuppositions and convictions that have contributed to Christian disunity in the first place.

Sacrament

Macquarrie published a synthesis of his theology of the sacraments in 1997, *A Guide to the Sacraments*.[38] In the preface, Macquarrie states the aim of the book very clearly: "My aim is to maintain the genuine mystery of the sacraments as means by which divine grace is mediated to us in this world of space and time and matter, but at the same time to get away from all magical and superstitious ideas about them." As well as this, he has an ecumenical aim "in the book's insistence that word and sacrament are inseparable or certainly ought to be."[39] This takes him beyond the traditional, and indeed superficial, Reformation divide: Catholic emphasis on sacrament, Protestant emphasis on word. For Macquarrie one may not be had without the other.

The Anglican priest-poet George Herbert is cited as summing up a natural theology of sacramentality: "Teach me, my God and King, in all things Thee to see." The goal of sacramental theology is to enable the experience of God's transparency and grace through created reality. This is a pervasive theme in Macquarrie. In the first edition of his *Paths in Spirituality* he points up the connection between "natural theology, the Incarnation, the Eucharist and the sacramental principle generally."[40] His conviction is that there must be some revelational consistency in the movement of God from creation through the Parousia. Protology and eschatology have an intrinsic teleological relationship. The incarnation is the center point, revealing the direction and meaning of this process, and anticipating its final fruition. Nor is this to be thought of as some Pelagian and necessary working out of the dynamics of nature and history: "[God] comes to us before we think of seeking him."[41] God's graceful and prior initiative demands not only a sense of his transcendence as the origin of all creation, but also a sense of his immanence in creation, his active dwelling within his world. God's immanent presence in creation may be fruitfully compared to Archbishop William Temple's analogy of the relation of an artist to his or her work, an analogy of which Macquarrie is quite fond. It occurs not only here in his *A Guide to the Sacraments,* but also in *The Humility of God.*[42] "The artist certainly transcends the work, for it is the artist who has created it. But the artist is bound to the work so created and has poured something of his own self into it so that from the work or through the work we can have a relation to the artist. Something of the artist is present in the work and revealed in the work." Thus the universal presence of God yields "a sacramental potentiality in virtually everything."[43] This does not mean, of course, that God is to be thought of as equally present or present with equal clarity in everything. The sacramental system of the church gives us the grace "to see God in some very dark phenomena." Although Macquarrie does not develop his thought immediately in this direction, perhaps we might say that the God who is encountered as omnipresent is the God most fully manifest in the person of our Lord Jesus Christ, and the shape of that supreme manifestation is cruciform. Christology (and soteriology) would then be a link between theology and sacramentality. Macquarrie wishes to avoid, at this point, a more narrow Christocentric construal of sacrament because of his explicit desire to secure the sacramental sense "in the very constitution of humanity." At the same time, since all creation without exception comes to be through Expressive Being, the Being of the Word that became enfleshed in Jesus, the potential of anything to be sacramental and the actuality of any sacrament is already to that extent Christocentric.

Sacramental Anthropology

Macquarrie will not let go of this universal religious sense in humankind, doing theology through anthropology. In the contemporary debates about nonfoundationalism, Macquarrie's position, in which is rooted the universal sacramental sense, is to acknowledge a general awareness of transcendence coextensive with human existence, and within this to recognize its supreme and unique expression in Jesus Christ and in the tradition of Christianity. If this universal religious experience is not to be dissolved, then we must not proceed too quickly or too immediately to Christian faith. This is not the place to argue Macquarrie's views over the nonfoundationalists, but simply to note how this universal sacramental consciousness is rooted.

Since we have access to the physical world both through our various senses and our rational minds, there is an appropriate fusion in the church's sacraments of the verbal and the nonverbal, of word and sign/symbol. If the verbal may be seen historically as more characteristic of the Reformation tradition, and the symbolic of the Catholic tradition, Macquarrie, as already noted, welcomes the narrowing of the ecumenical gap in recent times between these two ecclesial emphases.

Christ-Church-Sacrament

In respect of the institution of the sacraments by Jesus Christ Macquarrie notes approvingly the position of the *Catechism of the Catholic Church:* "As she has done for the canon of Sacred Scripture and for the doctrine of the faith, the Church, by the power of the Spirit who guides her 'into all truth,' has gradually recognized this treasure received from Christ and, as the faithful steward of God's mysteries, has determined its 'dispensation.'"[44] He distinguishes this position from what he sees as the more radical grounding of the sacraments in the person of Christ understood as the "primordial sacrament," a view associated with the influential Flemish Dominican theologian, Edward Schillebeeckx, O.P. Schillebeeckx's views have the merit of bringing together the entire sacramental sensibility, Christological-ecclesial and natural, in a certain hierarchy. "Christ is the sacrament of God; the church is the sacrament (body) of Christ; the seven sacraments are the sacraments of the church; the natural sacraments scattered around the world are, from a Christian point of view, approximations or pointers which find fulfillment in the sacraments of the gospel."[45] Here one may detect some advance over his earlier views on Christ as sacrament. In his book, *The Faith of the People of God: A Lay Theology*, Macquarrie distances himself somewhat from understanding Christ as sacrament or the church as sacrament.[46] Although curiously he does not make use of the idea of Christ as sacrament in his work *Jesus Christ in Modern Thought,* it is after this large work in Christology that he seems more favorably disposed to it.[47]

Macquarrie points out that the idea of Christ as the primordial sacrament at the center of the sacramental nexus is no new discovery, but "was obviously implicit from the beginning, and was occasionally made explicit." Perhaps it is first rendered explicit in Justin Martyr's *Logos Spermatikos,* but Macquarrie finds it clearly represented in the twentieth-century Anglican theologian Oliver Chase Quick (1885–1944), who wrote some fifty years before Schillebeeckx: "The life of Jesus Christ is seen as the perfect sacrament."[48] As the primordial sacrament, Christ may be seen as the true minister of the sacraments and, indeed, as their content. He is the Baptized One, whose faith is the ideal for every Christian; the Confirmed One, who expresses what it means to live out that baptismal vocation in deep and dedicated commitment; the Reconciler; the Really Present One; the Healer; the Priest; the Lover.

A Common Ordinal

In touching upon the validity of the sacraments, an obviously key concern in Roman Catholic theology, Macquarrie notes the common insistence of Catholics and Anglicans on episcopally ordained priests for the celebration of the eucharist. This has been a consistent concern for him, and yet at the same time he is aware of the Reformation tradition. In 1975, he advocated the use of a common ordinal that might bring the two Western ecclesial emphases together, Catholic and Protestant:

> As more and more groups might be persuaded to use it, then there would gradually grow up a ministry universally recognized, though differentiated according to the customs of the various churches. Such an ordinal, I assumed, would provide

for episcopal ordination, and one might hope that Roman Catholic bishops would eventually take part in the ordinations, so giving them a claim to wide recognition. In this way, the ordinal would be based on the Catholic substance of the doctrine of the ministry. But it would also incorporate whatever might seem of value in the Protestant principle, as applied to that doctrine.[49]

Is this an ecumenical pipe dream? One might develop a response to that question in a variety of ways. Clearly if one were to consider all denominations at this time that regarded themselves as in some way "Protestant," that would be an ecumenical pipe dream. If, however, one began to develop one's response with regard to the Anglican Communion, there is from the beginning a greater degree of realism. On the occasion of the canonization of forty martyrs, victims of the English Reformation, in 1970, Pope Paul VI declared:

> There will be no seeking to lessen the legitimate prestige and the worthy patrimony of piety and usage proper to the Anglican Church when the Roman Catholic Church—this humble "Servant of the servants of God"—is able to embrace her ever beloved sister in the one authentic Communion of the family of Christ, a communion of origin and of faith, a communion of priesthood and of rule, a communion of the saints in the freedom of love of the Spirit of Jesus."[50]

Pope Paul VI in this statement was not talking specifically about the Anglican Ordinal, but, at least implicitly, the pope admits the value of the Anglican "patrimony of piety and usage," including presumably the ordinal of the Book of Common Prayer. It is not impossible that an ordinal, acceptable to Catholics and Anglicans, might be developed as the ecumenical project continues.

Perhaps Macquarrie's point about a common ordinal in the context of statements like this is not at all far-fetched. Recently, Dr.

Rowan D. Williams, Macquarrie's immediate successor as the Lady Margaret Professor of Divinity at Oxford and now the Archbishop of Wales, has made suggestions with a strong family resemblance to Macquarrie's. At a meeting in May 2000 of Catholic and Anglican bishops to review the progress of the Anglican-Roman Catholic International Commission (ARCIC), Archbishop Williams suggested that the Christian churches should explore the possibility of "a pastoral ministry across a number of denominations." They could cooperate to ordain an ecumenical bishop with oversight over the shared ministries of variously determined ecumenical projects. According to Archbishop Williams, such a development is currently being planned in Wales among Anglican, Presbyterian, Baptist, United Reformed, and Methodist Churches. The archbishop was rightly uncertain if the Catholic Church would ever take part in such an undertaking—"Whether this will happen, I just don't know"—but he seems to believe that Catholic participation, even in the long run, would help sustain and solidify this important ecumenical step.[51] This appears to have all the substance of Macquarrie's proposal about a common ordinal and is actually planned to take place, albeit without Catholic participation.

Much has happened in ecumenism since 1975 but, if anything like the goals of classical ecumenism were regarded as desirable, it is difficult to see how they could be realized without proposals such as these. Macquarrie's theology will not dissolve or disallow the possibility of real and valid "doors to the sacred" in other churches. In this perspective, "validity" enables us to affirm that "grace is here." It does not entitle us to state absolutely where it is not.

Baptism and Confirmation

His consideration of baptism is very fine, but his treatment of confirmation leaves much to be desired. While there is some truth to the observation that confirmation remains a sacrament in search of a theology, much work has been done in recent years on the history and theology of this sacrament, for example, by the Anglican scholar J. D. C. Fisher and by the Catholics Aidan Kavanagh, O.S.B., Gerard Austin, O.P., and Paul Turner. Macquarrie shows no awareness of such contributions, so that his understanding of confirmation remains essentially unchanged from earlier studies.[52] Confirmation is for him the sacramental ratification of what took place in baptism, "a particularly solemn renewal in the presence of the church."[53] From a Catholic or Orthodox point of view, this is helpful, but not enough. To be more satisfactory, the account would need to move in the direction of something like "The Effects of Confirmation," as we have them in *The Catechism of the Catholic Church* (nos. 1302–3). Here confirmation is spelled out very clearly in relation to baptism:

> 1302 It is evident from its celebration that the effect of the sacrament of Confirmation is the special outpouring of the Holy Spirit as once granted to the apostles on the day of Pentecost.

> 1303 From this fact Confirmation brings an increase and deepening of baptismal grace: it roots us more deeply in the divine filiation which makes us cry, "Abba! Father!"; it unites us more firmly to Christ; it increases the gifts of the Holy Spirit in us; it renders our bond with the church more perfect; it gives us a special strength of the Holy Spirit to spread and defend the faith by word and action as true witnesses of Christ, to confess the name of Christ boldly, and never to be ashamed of the Cross.

Theologically Macquarrie would have no trouble endorsing this point of view, but it does not come to explicit expression in his work. This is an area of his theology where a more historically informed perspective would have been helpful.

Penance and Reconciliation

Macquarrie was invited by the Doctrine Commission of the Church of England to prepare a report on the sacrament of penance.[54] The report is vintage Macquarrie, as he moves from general considerations of penance and reconciliation, through a brief history of the tradition to some practical conclusions. Undoubtedly, one of the reasons for the invitation in the first place had to do with the clear articulation of the theology of the sacrament of penance in the revised edition of his *Principles of Christian Theology*.[55] One of his major concerns in both publications has been to emphasize the ecclesial and corporate nature of the sacrament. He thinks that the sacrament is seen as private and secret, and that it seems "to contradict the communal character which would appear to be needed in the sacraments of the church."[56] He is convinced that "The Church of today would appear less indulgent and more worthy of respect if it had a little more of the spirit of discipline—not indeed so harsh as at some times in the past, but with some more bite than there is at present, when virtually anything seems to be acceptable."[57]

Macquarrie's point could be better made by attending to the fruitful pastoral distinction in one and the same sacramental rite between "penance" and "reconciliation." While all Christians require ongoing penance as they are further conformed to the mind of Christ—"a little more of the spirit of discipline," in Macquarrie's words—fewer may require reconciliation, which presupposes that they have put themselves out of the communion of the church by their aware, free and deliberate action.

Anointing and Marriage

Macquarrie's treatment of the anointing of the sick is relatively brief but good. As is his philosophical wont, he discusses the interrelationship of mind and body, the meaning of health and wholeness, spiritual healing and physical healing. He recognizes along with the reformed rite of anointing of the sick of the Catholic Church that this is not exclusively a sacrament for the dying, but also for the sick. He emphasizes the helpful distinction between curing and healing:

> Curing has to do with relieving or removing the physical illness, whatever it may be....Healing belongs(s) to the entire person, body and soul. Unction does not guarantee cure. It may sometimes help toward a cure....But its aim is to heal the entire person. That could mean that although the physical condition is not cured, the sick person is enabled to integrate even his or her suffering into the personality and to become a better person in the process.[58]

There ought to be no avoidance of death, since it belongs to the finitude of our existence, and "this sacrament of unction can be understood as the bringing of the grace in which to face death...."[59]

In his treatment of the sacrament of marriage Macquarrie is particularly emphatic about the bond of marriage, a bond that has several strands.[60] The first of these strands is the *natural* one, arising out of the physical consummation of the marriage. This is a strand that obtains in any real marriage because "it affects the partners in the depth of their being, and may fairly be called ontological."[61] The next strand of the bond has to do with children, "one of the most powerful bonds in the marriage." The third strand is the *sacramental*. This is the strand of divine grace, blessing and supporting the marriage and formally expressed in the rite of marriage, either in prayers for the newly wed or in the eucharist. In his treatment of the bond or *vinculum* of marriage Macquarrie traces his typical theological methodology. He moves from more general concerns that have to do with humankind to the more specific concerns of the Christian community and refuses to allow any ontological distance between the two. The sacramental strand of the marriage bond is, if you will, a further degree of intensity explicitly opening the marriage to the transcendent presence of God. This further degree of intensity has to do with "the relation between Christ and his Church." The marriage becomes a "church in miniature," in which married people give themselves to one another in the grace of Christ, portraying in their lives the unique self-giving of Christ for the church.[62]

Holy Orders

Macquarrie's thoughts on the episcopate reflect the emphases found in Vatican Council II's *Christus Dominus,* the Decree on the Pastoral Office of Bishops in the Church. For Macquarrie the bishop is a teacher, a pastor, a sacramental figure and the leader of a diocese. He shows himself aware of the many demands made on a bishop in the contemporary church, but two comments stand out as of paramount importance. The first has to do with the bishop as teacher: "In modern times, it would be unrealistic to expect a bishop to be able to devote all his energies to theology, but he certainly should be aware of what is going on in theology if he is to fulfill his duty of maintaining and interpreting the apostolic faith."[63] The second comment notes how difficult it is in a large modern diocese for a bishop to fulfill his role as pastor. The bishop's pastoring of the pastors may be the best way for him to fulfill this role: "To whom can the purveyor of pastoral care turn, when he himself needs such care? Even in large dioceses, the bishop can still be a pastor to the pastors, so that he is still a pastor to the diocese, though indirectly." The profound ecclesial wisdom in these sentences needs no further comment.

He connects ordained ministry to baptism when he writes: "All have a ministry in the church of Christ, but not all have the same ministry."[64] He then emphasizes the permanent character of ordained ministry. The ministry of word and sacraments, embodied in ordination, is "the high point in a process that has already begun with that person's calling to the sacred ministry, and that will continue for a lifetime. Ordination is a lifelong vocation and commitment, and indeed it takes a lifetime for the full flourishing of a priestly character."[65] The character of ordination is given in the grace of the sacrament, but the formation and flourishing of that character remains the responsibility of a lifetime. This description of the flourishing of the sacramental character of ordination is borne out in the priest

John Macquarrie. It shines through his liturgical presidency, the care with which he celebrates the sacraments. During the week I was interviewing him at his Oxford home, on two occasions Macquarrie answered the telephone to respond to requests for him to take a funeral and to visit an old lady in the large hospital close to his home. On both occasions his response was positive, so that his theology of priesthood is not only clear on the pages of his books but is translucent in his person.

The Renewal of Anglicanism

In his foreword to Alister E. McGrath's *The Renewal of Anglicanism,* John Macquarrie writes that "There are few things, if any, that I long more to see than the renewal of Anglicanism."[66] There can be little doubt that Macquarrie has contributed to this renewal in his clear articulation of sacramental theology. In his *A Guide to the Sacraments* he has provided a worthy successor to Oliver Chase Quick's excellent *The Christian Sacraments,* first published in 1927. However, as will be evident from the survey in this chapter, he speaks not only to the renewal of Canterbury, but to the renewal of the entire *oikumene,* including Rome, and that is why Aidan Nichols, O.P., can say of him that "the orthodox Roman Catholic can recognize in him with but little effort a 'separated doctor' of the Catholic Church."[67] His sacramental theology, especially as found in his *A Guide to the Sacraments* is, in the words of Father David Forrester, Roman Catholic chaplain at Eton College, "Extremely informative, and obviously the product of deep faith and wide reading; it is a joy to read, written in a clear, concise, indeed lapidary style, and there is something in it for everyone."[68]

Pride in the Church

Distancing himself from any kind of ecclesial triumphalism, Macquarrie nonetheless believes that there is a right kind of pride in the church, a pride in the church's history or activities. "Such pride becomes sinful and blameworthy only when it settles into a hardened attitude of superiority or when it becomes egocentric and issues in an exclusive and contemptuous attitude to others."[69] Yet again this attitude exemplifies John Macquarrie himself. There is no attitude of superiority in the man, no egocentricity, no contempt of others. His ecclesiology and sacramental theology establish this to a fine degree. He knows that "The church shows, even if only weakly and fitfully, a hidden glory that is striving to find expression and realization," but it does show this glory. In 1970 Macquarrie wrote: "My personal love and admiration for the Roman Catholic Church, and my great commitment to the Catholic form of Christianity are great....I rejoice that even now we are so close to each other, and look forward to our drawing still closer together in the decades ahead."[70] If this is true of his theology of church and sacrament, it is even more true of his eucharistic theology, and to this we now turn.

CHAPTER 5

The Eucharist

The Jewel in the Crown

The eucharist is "the jewel in the crown," the "queen of the sacraments."[1] There is a purple passage in *Paths in Spirituality* that reveals the comprehensiveness, the depth and the richness of Macquarrie's eucharistic theology and that deserves to be quoted in full:

The Eucharist sums up in itself Christian worship, experience and theology in an amazing richness. It seems to include everything. It combines Word and Sacrament; its appeal is to spirit and to sense; it brings together the sacrifice of Calvary and the presence of the risen Christ; it is communion with God and communion with man; it covers the whole gamut of religious moods and emotions. Again, it teaches the doctrine of creation, as the bread, the wine and ourselves are brought to God; the doctrine of atonement, for these gifts have to be broken in order that they may be perfected; the doctrine of salvation, for the Eucharist has to do with incorporation into Christ and the sanctification of human life; above all, the doctrine of incarnation, for it is no distant God whom Christians worship but one who has made himself accessible in the world. The Eucharist also gathers up in itself the meaning of the Church; its whole action implies and sets forth our mutual interdependence in the body of Christ; it unites us with the Church of the past and even, through its paschal overtones, with the first people of God, as an anticipation of the heavenly banquet. Comprehensive though this description is, it is likely that I have missed something out, for the Eucharist seems to be inexhaustible.[2]

If ever a statement were needed, demonstrating clearly the integration of eucharistic belief and theology with the entire fabric of Christian doctrine, this is it. The eucharist is related to all of life and theology. At the same time, he notes that in the history of the Christian tradition there have been different emphases on various aspects of the eucharist. This is almost impossible to avoid, but "it is only wrong when one aspect is stressed to the exclusion of others, and this has sometimes happened."[3] To avoid such forms of exclusion Macquarrie deliberately sets out to articulate eucharistic theology in a way that would be acceptable to "most of the major communions of the Christian Church."[4]

This interpretation of the sacrament, consonant with his systematic theology as a whole, is in existential-ontological terms. This way of proceeding is typically expressive of the *via media anglicana*. As existential, the eucharistic reality cannot be understood in purely objective terms and cannot be an event that takes place *extra nos*. As ontological, the eucharistic reality cannot be founded on any merely subjective appreciation of the sacrament. "The Eucharist is decidedly not a mere memorial or a way of helping us to remember what Christ did a long time ago. It is a genuine re-presenting of Christ's work. In this sacrament, as in the others, the initiative is with God; it is he who acts in the sacrament and makes himself present."[5] From a traditional Catholic point of view, Macquarrie's perspective tensively holds together the *ex opere operato* and the *ex opere operantis* dimensions of the sacrament.

The Eucharistic Sacrifice

While he obviously distances himself from viewing the eucharist as a memorial of Christ in a subjectivist sense, curiously there seems to be in his earlier theology a degree of ambivalence in Macquarrie's handling of the notion of memorial/*anamnesis*. On the one hand, he seems to fault the Anglican-Roman Catholic International Commission's *Windsor Statement on the Eucharist* of 1971:

> …for some reason ARCIC was very biblicist in its treatment of the eucharist. Thus the difficult notions of eucharistic sacrifice and eucharistic presence were made to rest very largely on a highly dynamic exegesis of the Greek word *anamnesis,* "memorial." The exegesis may be correct, but there are scholars who contest it, and *by itself* it provides an insecure base for what ARCIC wanted to say.[6]

This is an unnecessarily harsh interpretation of ARCIC's use of *anamnesis,* which is not faulted by the formal "Responses" of the Church of England or of the Catholic Bishops of England and Wales. In fact, the only dissenting scholar that Macquarrie presents is the Evangelical Anglican Philip E. Hughes.

On the other hand, in his more recent *Jesus Christ in Modern Thought* he develops a much more favorable reaction to *anamnesis,* this time relying especially upon the contribution of Joachim Jeremias: "A further point made by Jeremias and again commonly accepted by liturgical scholars, is that *anamnesis* does not mean just a remembering of the past, 'God's remembrance is never a simple remembering of something, but always an effecting and creating event.'"[7] Thus Macquarrie ends up with an interpretation of *anamnesis* more consistent with his existential-ontological methodology. The Christian assembly remembers, that is, represents, the unique saving action of Christ in the eucharist, but the foundation of the assembly's remembering is the efficacious, creative "remembrance" of God. Macquarrie's understanding here is entirely consonant with the expression and meaning of ARCIC's *Windsor Statement,* paragraph 5:

> The notion of *memorial* as understood in the Passover celebration at the time of Christ—i.e., the making effective in

the present of an event in the past—has opened the way to a clear understanding of the relationship between Christ's sacrifice and the Eucharist. The eucharistic memorial is no mere calling to mind of a past event or its significance, but the Church's effectual proclamation of God's mighty acts.

Macquarrie's treatment of eucharistic sacrifice is quite brief in contrast to his consideration of the real presence of Christ. With respect to eucharistic sacrifice, Macquarrie sees its origins immediately in the events of the Last Supper and the death of Christ. Ultimately, however, sacrifice means self-giving, and self-giving is characteristic of the very life and existence of God: "He is the God who is always coming out from himself in love and sharing and self-giving, and the commitment that he makes to his creation already points forward to the fuller involvement of the incarnation and the passion."[8] The people of God realizes itself to the extent that it takes into and is formed by this divine self-giving, that is, by eucharist. This sacrificial self-giving is simultaneously the ultimate realization of human potential, not in a Pelagian sense, but in the sense of surrender to and conformity with the very being of God. The sacrifice of the eucharist is the ritual focus that unites protology and eschatology, Christology and ecclesiology, and each one of these doctrines is but comment on the Self-Giving that the mystery of the Trinity is.

Within the eucharistic rite itself two moments especially touch on the ideal of sacrifice: the offertory (the offering of the bread and wine before the consecration), and the oblation (the offering of those elements after the consecration). In the offertory the bread and wine stand for the people of the assembly themselves as they cooperate with and submit to God in response to the initiative of God's self-giving, proclaimed in the Liturgy of the Word. In contrast, the oblation "is done by the priest alone, for in this he is acting in Christ's place, and this means that it is Christ who makes the oblation."[9] This affirmation that the priest is acting in Christ's place takes Macquarrie into a consideration of ordained ministry through the notion of "character," but in a particularly nuanced fashion.

He eschews a purely functionalist approach to ordination. He insists that the ordained ministers are not simply persons authorized to perform specific functions within the church, but that there is an ontological dimension to ordination, traditionally designated by the word "character."[10] "Character" is best understood as a formation and pattern of personal being. "It is through the doing of acts that character is formed, then character in turn informs the acts." The character of baptism and confirmation is not instantly injected into the person, as if in some magical way. Christians grow into the character of their baptism and confirmation, initiated on the day of ritual celebration. The character of ordination is to be understood similarly. "Priesthood is a lifetime commitment and a lifelong vocation, and indeed takes the best part of a lifetime for the full flowering of priestly character."[11] What has been referred to traditionally as the indelibility of the character expresses primarily God's faithfulness to his enabling grace and consequently, the irreversibility of the process initiated by ordination. The fact that the process may be arrested or not exercised by some of the ordained cannot detract from the self-giving faithfulness of God in the act of ordination. While, however, the ministry of the ordained remains distinctive within the church, it is integrated into and is continuous with the general ministry of all the baptized.

Nowhere in Macquarrie's corpus can one find any very detailed account of Anglican debate about eucharistic sacrifice such as that of the late Bishop Richard P. C. Hanson and (now Archbishop of Wales) Rowan Williams.[12] Hanson, an acknowledged expert in patristic theology, combed the patristic period with reference to eucharistic sacrifice. His views reflect the Reformed perspective of evangelical Anglicanism: "I do not see how the primitive and central doctrine of the collective priesthood of all believers [or of all the baptized] can seriously be thought to be consistent with the doctrine of a priestly class empowered to control eucharistic sacrifice."[13] Williams, in his response to Hanson's "impeccably documented survey" is complementary rather than contradictory, but represents an Anglo-Catholic position.[14] He emphasizes the uniqueness of Christ's sacrifice on the cross, the role of the priest "in the person of Christ," and the re-presentational act of the eucharist. Hanson and Williams are a contemporary expression of the ongoing tension on eucharistic sacrifice that made itself present in Anglicanism in the sixteenth century. Macquarrie is aware of the tension, but does not enter into the minutiae of patristic and medieval theology. The only reasonable conclusion is that he viewed the matter sufficiently explored and resolved within the frame of his own theology and therefore that it required no further comment. Unlike Hanson and Williams, Macquarrie seems to have little time for the nuances and subtleties of historical theology on this particular issue. His methodological bias is avowedly philosophical but careful, even if brief attention to the historical evolution of the doctrine of eucharistic sacrifice would both enhance and strengthen his already solid judgment. In a private communication, Macquarrie indicated to me that he had considered in some detail historical dimensions of eucharistic sacrifice and a sacrificing priesthood in the second edition of *Paths in Spirituality* and *A Guide to the Sacraments.*[15] This is absolutely true, but the point is, however, that his historical reflections deal almost exclusively with the Reformation-period debate concerning eucharistic sacrifice. A more penetrating patristic and medieval study, like Hanson-Williams, would have made his already very fine position even more suasive. The brilliance of his rooting of eucharistic sacrifice in the reality of God as Self-Gift, reaching its climactic expression in Christ's sacrifice, re-presented in the eucharist, could be anchored in historical narrative that would push the question back long before the Reformation made it a singularly divisive issue. But perhaps this is asking Macquarrie to be omnicompetent.

Eucharistic Presence

God is acknowledged in the Christian tradition to be universally present to his creation, and Jesus Christ as the divine Logos/Word is, therefore, also universally present.[16] How is this acknowledgment of the universal presence of the triune God to be reconciled with the idea of a particular presence, for example, in the incarnation, in the church, in the sacraments? Macquarrie's response is to affirm that it would be virtually impossible to recognize the universal presence if there were no particular presences:

> It is very important not to let particular presences be simply swallowed up in a universal presence. I doubt very much whether such a universal presence could ever be detected or recognized unless we were pointed to it by particular presences, moments of intensity, of meeting or encounter. It is part of our human nature to seek those particular occasions.[17]

Thus, in the Old Testament, the ark of the covenant, the tabernacle, the temple, the *shekinah* are to be understood as centers that focused with intensity God's universal presence for the ancient Hebrews.

With regard to the eucharist, just as the entire celebration falls into two distinct parts, the Liturgy of the Word and the Liturgy of the Eucharist, so the recognition of Christ's presence takes this twofold shape. In the Liturgy of the Word, the climax of this recognition is the proclamation of the Gospel. In the Liturgy of the Eucharist the climax occurs in the consecrated elements.[18] Secondly, Macquarrie sees the congregation's response to the presence in the word coming in the communal affirmation of the creed, and the presence in the consecrated elements in the reception of holy communion. Finally, two ritual gestures express in a parallel fashion this dual mode of Christ's presence: the elevation of the book of the Gospels and the elevation of the eucharistic gifts.[19]

In speaking of the body of Christ care must be taken to note the threefold significance of the term. Literally, the term applies to the "actual personal being-in-the-world" of the historical Jesus of Nazareth, the body he took from the womb of the Virgin Mary. The body of Christ is also the sacramental host, representing Christ and received in holy communion. The body of Christ is at the same time the worshiping assembly, incorporated into Christ through baptism and confirmation, "and now being steadily conformed to him through participation in the Eucharist."[20]

After commenting on the eucharistic presence of Christ as temporal and as spiritual, Macquarrie opts for the category of "personal presence" as the most appropriate. Personal presence is not, however, to be construed as synonymous with purely "spiritual" presence, because "a person is embodied and includes a physical presence."[21] His notion of personal presence transcends the typical representation of the subject-object pattern. Personal presence is objective-ontological because it entirely depends on the initiative of Holy Being epiphanied in particular beings, the eucharistic elements of bread and wine. At the same time, the presence is just as much subjective-existential, insofar as this particular manifestation of Holy Being occurs only in the context of the body of Christ, understood in the polyvalent sense noted above. Here again is seen the continuous application of Macquarrie's existential-ontological theism.

As with all personal presence, the personal presence of Christ in the eucharist is multidimensional. Christ is present in his body, the community, the presiding minister, the word as well as in the consecrated elements. "Christ is present par excellence in the consecrated bread and wine."[22] Macquarrie warns about trying to fix a "moment of consecration" too precisely, insisting that "the whole prayer of consecration consecrates."

This multidimensional personal presence of Christ in the eucharist has been expounded in various theories employing philosophical categories such as "substance," "significance," "value." The central issue is belief in a real, abiding eucharistic presence, but a degree of theological pluralism in articulating this belief is both permissible and desirable.

Macquarrie gives attention to substance/transubstantiation and significance/transsignification. He does not give the same degree of exposure to "transvaluation," a eucharistic theory that enjoyed some success in the Church of England. The Anglican lay theologian, Sir Will Spens, seems to have been the first to advance a view of eucharistic presence in terms of value-philosophy, but he was overshadowed by the more famous Archbishop William Temple in his illuminating *Christus Veritas*.[23] He notes that the doctrine of transubstantiation has been dominant in the Western church for a long time. He considers it historically important as "the official eucharistic theology of the Roman Catholic Church…even if it is no longer held to be explanatory," though he does not subscribe to it himself.[24] Distancing himself from Protestant polemicists, Macquarrie affirms that transubstantiation has absolutely nothing to do with a magical approach to the eucharist and, in fact, is best regarded as one of the solid defenses against such a position. According to this theory of eucharistic presence, there is no sensible difference whatsoever in the eucharistic elements before and after consecration. "Physics and chemistry have got nothing to do with what happens in consecration; or, to put it in different language, one could never get any empirical verification of the presence of Christ in the consecrated elements."[25] The presence of Christ is perceptible only to the eyes of faith, to a seeing "in depth," and Macquarrie is fond of citing the words of St. Thomas Aquinas from the hymn "Tantum ergo": "faith, our outward sense befriending" enables us to perceive the divine eucharistic presence.[26]

While St. Thomas may be the architect of transubstantiation, it does not originate with him. While the term had been used occasionally, it was first officially sanctioned by the Fourth Lateran Council in 1215: "The body and blood (of Jesus Christ) are truly contained in the sacrament of the altar, under the appearances of bread and wine, the bread being transubstantiated into the body by the divine power and the wine into the blood.…"[27] The statement of the council, in Macquarrie's judgment, is careful, especially the emphasis that the transformation comes about "by divine power." It was St. Thomas, however, who was to flesh out the details of the meaning of "substance." For St. Thomas, "substance" is a metaphysical term, not to be identified with physical matter. For St. Thomas the accidents of bread and wine remain unchanged. "Substance" language, therefore, affirms a doctrine of eucharistic presence that is realistic without being materialistic or physicalist. When, however, the austere language of the Lateran Council and of St. Thomas is set alongside the statement about transubstantiation from the Council of Constance in 1417, against the opinions of Wyclif and Hus, there have occurred some significant changes. In the decrees of Constance we read: "After the consecration of the priest in the sacrament of the altar under the covering of bread and wine there is not material bread and material wine but Christ himself...."[28] As Macquarrie interprets this language, there is reference here not to a metaphysical change of substance, but rather substance has been identified with physical matter. Material bread and wine have been "replaced" by the body and blood of Christ. Furthermore, the transformation is not effected "by divine power" but "after the consecration of the priest." The originally austere doctrine of transubstantiation had degenerated into "the semimagical teaching that the Reformers knew as transubstantiation and that they rejected, as in Article 28 of the *Book of Common Prayer*."[29] The real defect of the eucharistic language of Constance in Macquarrie's judgment is the denial of the sacramental-incarnational principle whereby material realities become ontologically the presence of the divine, but without ceasing to be material realities. The Reformers latched on to the defective or corrupt form of transubstantiation but failed to advert to the earlier, more positive forms of the doctrine.

The Council of Trent is more in harmony with the earlier form of transubstantiation than the Council of Constance. While Trent affirms a real or substantial change in the eucharistic elements, this is never teased out too precisely. The "how" of Christ's presence in the eucharist is not explained, and "it is simply claimed that the word [transubstantiation] is one that may be suitably used, and has been so used by the church."[30] Macquarrie rightly sees this approach to transubstantiation reflected in the ARCIC Agreed Statement on the Eucharist.

While genuinely appreciative of transubstantiation, Macquarrie is also critical of the term. He takes notice of Edward Schillebeeckx's interpretation of Trent: "At Trent the word 'transubstantiation' explained nothing, but simply stood for the Catholic as against the

Protestant understanding of the Eucharist."[31] This is firstly an over-simplification because there is no one Protestant way of understanding the eucharist. Secondly, however, if the word simply affirms a "real presence" of Christ in the eucharist without any explanatory theory (the "how" of that presence), then the term is quite misleading. It is misleading because it suggests the entire Aristotelian-Thomist philosophical apparatus of hylomorphism, and "this philosophical apparatus is not one that readily recommends itself today."[32] His own existential-ontological view understands the world not as "an aggregate of substances, but as a structure of meaning."[33] Finally, Macquarrie considers the language of hylomorphism inappropriate because it is impersonal language, whereas the language of eucharistic presence is best understood, as we have seen, in personal terms.

Another theological theory just as capable as transubstantiation of sustaining a deep and rich eucharistic faith and practice, is transsignification. The philosophical backdrop of this theory is the phenomenological and existentialist categories of Husserl, Merleau-Ponty, and Heidegger. In this philosophical tradition reality is not constituted by "thinghood" or we might say "substance," but by "a personally structured totality of meanings."[34] This does not render reality the construal of the subject, finally expressed as some form of idealism. Rather, the linguistic and significant community, of which the individual is part and to which he contributes, determines meaning and reality. This is central to Macquarrie's existential-ontological theism and seems to bear a strong family resemblance to the postliberal theology of George A. Lindbeck. The linguistic-cultural perspective of the individual is established through and by a linguistic-cultural community, in this instance the church.[35] Macquarrie writes:

> The effect of the language (of the eucharistic action) is to shift the elements out of the one region of signification into another—from the everyday world into the setting of the eucharistic community. This is not a subjective view of presence, if one accepts that significance enters into the onto-

logical constitution of a thing; but neither is it an objective view, as if the body and blood of Christ existed outside the context of he eucharistic community, which is also his body.[36]

Macquarrie does not maintain that his version of existential-ontological theism applied to eucharistic presence is identical with transsignification as understood by Catholic scholars, but only that it is "close to" it and is preferable to transubstantiation. For Macquarrie, "no theory of eucharistic presence can ever be more than an approximation,"[37] which could well stand as a twentieth-century paraphrase of what the Anglican divine Lancelot Andrewes said to Cardinal Robert Bellarmine: "We believe no less than you that the presence is real, but concerning the mode of that presence we define nothing rashly."[38]

Eucharistic Reservation

"What happens to the consecrated elements at the end of the Eucharist? What people do with them is often a good guide to what theology of presence they hold."[39] If this axiom is applied to John Macquarrie, then what emerges is a very high theology of presence indeed. He maintains that the primary aim of reservation is the communion of the sick and of those unable to attend the eucharist, and he is aware that this practice may be traced back to Justin Martyr and the *Apostolic Tradition*.[40] Yet, reservation for the sick cannot be isolated and includes latent possibilities for devotion: "For the sacrament cannot be retained or reserved in a merely casual way, as if one could be resolved to take a precious gift to the sick and yet be also resolved to treat that gift lightly."[41] A proper reverence for the reserved eucharist may issue in personal prayer and devotion, the kind of devotion that seeks to extend the eucharist to all of life that it may be conformed to its living Lord. The key eucharistic devotional practice is Benediction, of which Macquarrie is a staunch advocate. "Psychologically speaking we need some concrete visible manifestation toward which to direct our devotion; while theologically speaking, this is already provided for us by our Lord's gracious manifestation of his presence in the Blessed Sacrament."[42]

Conclusion

Macquarrie writes of theologians: "Theologians can only too easily begin to think of themselves as the *teleoi* (the perfect), those who attained to a *gnosis* (knowledge) that is beyond the reach of the ordinary faithful."[43] This is not a temptation to which John Macquarrie himself has succumbed. John S. Bowden, Macquarrie's publisher and editor at the Student Christian Movement Press in London, has this to say about him: "He has proved a successful mediator between the academic world and the parishes in producing a believing form of academic theology."[44] It is fashionable today to speak of theology having three publics—the church, the academy, and society—but perhaps less fashionable to see theology in the academy serving the faith of the church. If Bowden is correct, then John Macquarrie has consistently tried to serve the faith of the church, and the church understood in the widest sense, in its catholicity, and not only his own Anglican Communion. His eucharistic theology serves well his own ecclesial tradition, but it speaks powerfully to Rome and Geneva as well as to Canterbury. He knows, respects, and loves the eucharistic tradition, and yet in his retrieval of it he is critical. The cause of ecumenism is advanced not only through official, ecclesial dialogues, but also through the creative, careful mediation of theology to worshiping communities by theologians like John Macquarrie.

CHAPTER 6

Mary

In his ecumenical Marian theology, Father George H. Tavard has a fine chapter entitled "Mary in Anglicanism," in which he traces the development of Marian teaching from Thomas Cranmer to the present. Tavard's essay is not intended to be comprehensive and so, while he maintains that it would be "an exaggeration to speak of a Marian movement in contemporary Anglicanism," nonetheless significant contributions have been made in recent times, for example, by Donald Allchin, John Macquarrie, and the late Norman Pittenger.[1] These three Anglican theologians make an interesting contrast. Allchin has a particularly strong ecumenical sense and an equally strong sense of the development of the Anglican tradition of theology and spirituality.[2] *The Joy of All Creation: An Anglican Meditation on the Place of Mary* is an outstanding example of Allchin's ability to read the Anglican tradition, drawing out its richness for today. He is at his best in this kind of fruitful historical probing. His mining of the seventeenth-century Anglican divines' teaching about Mary stands on its own. This kind of historical investigation is not in the forefront of Macquarrie's theological strengths. He is best compared to someone like the process theologian Norman Pittenger, as we shall see.

Mary and Vatican Council II

Three factors have combined to shape Mariological reflection in the thirty-five years since the end of Vatican Council II: *Lumen Gentium,* ecumenical dialogue, and new theological movements. At

the time of the council, there was some interest in developing a separate document on the Mother of God, but the majority of the
council fathers wanted reflection on Mary to constitute an integral
part of reflection on the church. Thus, the final chapter of *Lumen
Gentium,* the Constitution on the Church, is given over to "Our
Lady."[3] Mary is hailed "as preeminent and as a wholly unique member of the Church, and as its type and outstanding model in faith and
charity."[4] The Constitution goes on to describe the Virgin Mary's
role in the history of salvation and treats briefly of the immaculate
conception and assumption. It insists with the tradition that "there is
but one mediator" and that "Mary's function as mother of men in
no way obscures or diminishes this unique mediation of Christ, but
rather shows its power."[5] Finally, after advocating the legitimate cult
of the Blessed Virgin, "especially the liturgical cult," the Constitution
ends with Mary as "sign of true hope and comfort for the pilgrim
people of God."[6]

Since Vatican II the entry of the Catholic Church into the ecumenical movement has further contributed to a renewal of Mariology.
It is true, as claimed recently by the veteran ecumenical theologian,
the Methodist Geoffrey Wainwright, that "Mary has not so far been
the subject of sustained treatment in any modern international bilat-
eral or multilateral dialogue," but that does not mean that there has
been no ecumenical advance on the subject.[7] The celebrated ecumenical volume, *Mary in the New Testament,* is one of the best examples of this kind of cooperation.[8] The various contributors to this
volume establish very clearly "the plurality and ambiguity of biblical
portraits of Mary."[9] The Ecumenical Society of the Blessed Virgin
Mary, founded by the late Martin Gillett, is another example of ecumenical progress. This society was born in Brussels in 1966 during cel-
ebrations of the fortieth anniversary of the completion of the Malines
Conversations (1921–26), unofficial ecumenical exchanges between
Anglicans and Catholics. The society held its first official meeting in
1967 in London and has produced various anthologies of essays on
Marian theology. The upshot of these ecumenical essays is to extend
the understanding of Mary across the ecumenical divide.[10]

Third, various movements in theology have had their own impact on the development of Marian theology, for example, feminism and liberation theology. Macquarrie notes: "The new interest in the feminine and the belief that God has for too long been presented in exclusively masculine terms is also leading to a new awareness of Mary and a willingness to reconsider her place in theology...."[11] In the former category one might think of Elizabeth Johnson's recent work, especially her *Friends of God and Prophets: A Feminist Theological Reading of the Communion of Saints*,[12] or Maurice Hamington's book, *Hail Mary? The Struggle for Ultimate Womanhood in Catholicism*.[13] Such works challenge the received view of Mary informed by patriarchal presuppositions and search for new, liberating understandings of Mary. For liberation theology, Leonardo Boff's *The Maternal Place of God* is an example of a liberationist theology of Mary.[14] Liberation theologians try to see the potential of Mary, not least in the Magnificat, for a nonoppressive and more just approach to social issues in Latin America and Asia especially. Macquarrie is no advocate of feminist or liberation theology, though he has acknowledged some of their values. Rather he tends to respond to more traditional doctrinal categories for Mary, and brings out of his treasury new things and old.

The Mysteries of Mary

In *Principles of Christian Theology* Macquarrie treats of Mary in that chapter devoted to ecclesiology. "No ecumenical theology could afford to ignore [mariology]."[15] He recognizes right away that his inclusion of this topic in a book on systematics may stir a negative reaction among those of a Protestant background, and so immediately he reassures by saying that his treatment will be roundly based on Holy Scripture, respecting the *sola scriptura* emphasis of the Reformation tradition.[16]

If one begins with Scripture one sees that the discovery of the "historical Mary" is even more fraught with problems and difficulties than the "historical Jesus." In the Gospel records as we now have them the narrative is a mixture of historical and legendary material. The data presented offer us truths of faith, not raw historical fact, and perhaps are best designated as "mysteries."[17] Macquarrie considers three of these Marian mysteries: the annunciation, the visitation and the station at the cross. The annunciation, emphasizing the initiative of God, reveals the incarnation taking place through the action of the Holy Spirit. It has also a contemporary meaning in that something similar happens in and to the church: "…for just as (Mary) was the bearer of the Christ, so the church, his body, brings christhood into the world…through the action of the Holy Spirit…."[18] The visitation of Mary to Elizabeth was the occasion for the great canticle of the Magnificat. The key word in the canticle is "blessed." Blessed among women, according to Elizabeth's greeting and blessed by all generations, Mary is indeed the blessed one. Her blessedness, however, "adumbrates the blessedness of the church—no earthly happiness, but a 'likeness to God' which means a participation in God's self-giving love…."[19] Mary's blessedness in the visitation mystery is a type also of the blessedness of the church. It expresses something of the church's vocation. The third mystery, Mary's station at the cross, also contains an ecclesial aspect. Relying on an insight of the Danish theologian-philosopher, Søren Kierkegaard, Macquarrie points out that Mary's suffering is not to be understood "as only a natural grief at the sight of Jesus' death, but as a sharing in his self-emptying, as if Mary were experiencing something of what Christ expressed in his cry of dereliction; and Mary's suffering is experienced in turn by every disciple…."[20] In these three mysteries Mary is closely linked to the church, and this is where, according to Macquarrie, she is best understood.

The best clue to the scriptural understanding of Mary is the title given to her by Pope Paul VI, "Mother of the Church." This title, Macquarrie believes, provides an opening on which Catholics, Orthodox, Anglicans, and Protestants may agree. It is an ecumenically accessible title for Mary. Its scriptural basis may be found on the lips of Jesus on the cross, "Woman behold your son….Behold your mother!" (John 19.26). Behind the title there lie two meanings. First, it accords to Mary "a certain priority in the church, as one who played an indispensable role in the Christian drama of incarnation and salvation."[21] The second meaning behind the title is Mary as the prototype of the church: "What we see in Mary, we ought to see in the church."[22]

The Immaculate Conception and the Assumption of Mary

Macquarrie turns his attention in a particularly fruitful way to the two Marian dogmas of the immaculate conception and the assumption of Mary into heaven. "When purged of mythological elements, (they) can be interpreted as implications of more central Christian teaching."[23] Here too for Macquarrie there is a connection between Mary and the church.

He finds the language of Pope Pius IX's 1854 constitution promulgating the immaculate conception, *Ineffabilis Deus,* unhelpful: "We declare…that the most blessed Virgin Mary in the first moment of her conception was, by the unique grace and privilege of God, in view of the merits of Jesus Christ the Saviour of the human race, preserved intact from all stain of original sin." The language is unhelpful in that the image of sin as "stain" is too impersonal, and the emphasis on Mary's being "preserved" from original sin is too negative.[24] A fresh approach to the dogma needs to be found. One might go beyond the quasiphysical understanding of sin as stain by suggesting sin as alienation or estrangement. A person "preserved" from original sin, then, would be one whose life "has not been stunted and distorted by the alienation of the race."[25] But there is more to it than that. The immaculate conception affirms that the "original righteousness" of humankind was not totally wiped out by "original sin." There is grace in creation, a grace nurtured and strengthened in Israel and reaching its high point in the receptivity of Mary to the gift of the incarnation. "The moment had come when alienation was at an end, when mankind had been brought to the condition of being *capax Dei,* capable of receiving God in the gift of the incarnation."[26]

The assumption into heaven shows Mary, "the perfect type of the church," taken up by Christ to share his heavenly existence.[27] Macquarrie indicates that the assumption of Mary is dependent upon the ascension of Christ, and not simply its parallel: "The assumption of the blessed Virgin is dependent upon the ascension of Jesus Christ; it is indeed a corollary of it because of the glorification of human nature in him."[28] Or, as put by Karl Rahner, S.J., "The [ascended Jesus Christ] did not go to a ready-made heaven that was awaiting him, rather he created heaven, understood as a nexus of personal relations."[29] Primary place in this heaven belongs to the woman whose assent became the vehicle for the consummation of God's graceful plan for humankind. The assumption is the transformation of Mary from her familiar earthly state to a new mode of being in which she enjoys a perfected and immediate relation to God. Since that perfected state is the hope of all Christians, what Mary enjoys through the assumption is the hope for each and every Christian: "It is not just a personal dogma about Mary (though it is that) but a dogma about the church, the whole body of the faithful of whom Mary is the type. Mary's glorious assumption, we may say, is the first moment in the glorious assumption of the church."[30]

Macquarrie consistently refuses to sever the connection between Mary and the church so that virtually everything that is said of Mary may be said of the church, and, therefore, of the individuals who constitute the church. Mariology in that precise sense is not a discrete theological discipline, but interfaces with Christology, anthropology, ecclesiology. A New York colleague of Macquarrie's, though at General Theological Seminary rather than Union Theological Seminary, was the late Norman Pittenger. Though their theological methodology is in some ways very close—both, for example, find classical metaphysics no longer useful or helpful, and a processive type of metaphysics more intelligible to modern people— Macquarrie is more thorough and consistent in acknowledging the connections between Mary and the church than Pittenger.

Norman Pittenger and Mariology

Norman Pittenger, born in 1905 and who was in retirement and until his death in 1997 senior resident at King's College, the University of Cambridge, has been a prolific Anglican theologian. His ninetieth and last book was on Marian theology and devotion, *Our Lady: The Mother of Jesus in Christian Faith and Devotion,* and offers a good contrast to Macquarrie's Mariology.[31] Like Macquarrie in his ability and commitment to mediate academic theology to the general public of the church, Pittenger has the same gift. Dean Lawrence Rose of General Theological Seminary, New York City, where Pittenger worked all his life, said of him: "Many of his writings have been 'popular' in the best possible sense of the word—for people—designed to bring the truth of Christianity out of the cloister or the study and give it currency in the living thought of men and women today."[32] While Macquarrie found the philosophical apparatus of Martin Heidegger offering him a conceptuality in which to articulate for modern people the Christian faith, Pittenger's project of making Christian theology accessible to people led him to a growing appreciation of process thought, especially to the writings of Alfred North Whitehead and Charles Hartshorne. He has presented over the years almost the entire fabric of Christian doctrine in process conceptual categories. His book on Mary also contains a very clear précis of process theology.[33] His theological portrait of Mary, however, is not substantially dependent upon process thought. He has a solid acquaintance with the entire sweep of the Christian tradition. Because of his lucidity and the suasive charm and style of his writing, his book on Mary is close to Macquarrie's. Macquarrie's Mariology is intended to have a broad ecumenical appeal, and Pittenger advocates a "chastened" Mariology that he sees as typically Anglican, valuing both the Catholic-Orthodox and the Reformation emphases of the Christian tradition.

Commenting on the apocryphal literature about Mary (the Infancy Gospel of Thomas, the Arabic Gospel of the Childhood, the History of Joseph the Carpenter, the Protevangelium of James),

Pittenger considers them the products "of a devout but highly fanciful imagination whose details are of no significance for Christian faith…."[34] Macquarrie would be in agreement with Pittenger when he sees such literature as the stuff of sheer legend. Pittenger distinguishes such legend from what he calls genuine myth and into this latter category he places Mary as the second Eve, the perpetual virginity of Mary, the immaculate conception, and the assumption of Mary into heaven. These are all classified as "Mariological mythology." The difference between myth and legend for him is that in the latter category the pious imagination seems "to have run riot."[35] While there are aspects of his judgment about the apocryphal literature that ring true, it is unfortunate that Pittenger categorizes the immaculate conception and the assumption without further ado as "Mariological mythology." Apart from the somewhat misleading terminology he employs, there seems to be no awareness on his part, as there is in Macquarrie, of the profound anthropological and ecclesial insights in the Marian dogmas.

Furthermore, Pittenger actually provides, and from an angle missing in Macquarrie, a basis for the doctrine of the immaculate conception when he describes so finely the influence Mary had on her son, Jesus. He gives particular emphasis to her maternal role in the formation of her son: "…as a mother whose son himself was a man of faith, we can see that her attitude and her way of behaving was of the sort which follows when we recognize that a son is influenced and affected by his parents and *above all by his mother*."[36] The question rises naturally, "What must she herself have been like to have nurtured a son like that?" Arguably, we find in such observations the seeds of the doctrine of the immaculate conception, an inductive approach to the doctrine, as it were. Such a point of view may be found in an earlier Cambridge Anglican theologian, Harry A. Williams, who wrote of the immaculate conception in this vein: "The Roman Church, in declaring our Lady to be born without taint of original sin, gave expression in a theological idiom to what Freud later discovered in his consulting-room—the overwhelming influence for good or bad which a mother has upon her infant and child."[37]

Like Macquarrie Pittenger emphasizes that Mary is a type of the church, and he sees this fully developed in the annunciation. He does not use Macquarrie's favored term "mystery" for the event, and, indeed, is explicitly quite skeptical of the historical details surrounding the annunciation. Nonetheless, the annunciation is replete with theological insights: "The annunciation story may be dubiously historical both in detail and in background, yet perhaps it is telling us something that within the Christian tradition of faith, worship and life is of quite enormous significance."[38] Given that in the process conceptuality all divine activity in creation is dependent upon creaturely responsiveness to the divine initiative or lure, Mary's fiat may be seen as "precisely a supreme symbolic instance of consent to the divine will."[39] Her entirely appropriate yet free response to the divine initiative made known to her through the angel Gabriel makes her "a model for all genuine Christian discipleship."[40] Mary typifies the faith-filled Christian response for the individual and for the body corporate, the response of receptivity and openness.[41]

Conclusion

Even in a very obviously Catholic discipline like Mariology, John Macquarrie shows a remarkable openness to the broad Catholic tradition. He evinces a concern to retrieve traditional Marian doctrines by presenting them in a fashion that makes them more intelligible to people today, and he has been very successful. Introducing Macquarrie's *Mary for All Christians,* his colleague in the Ecumenical Society of the Blessed Virgin Mary, Dom Alberic Stacpoole, O.S.B., stated that "We have been blessed by all our members, not least Oxford's former Lady Margaret Professor."[42] This chapter establishes some of the reasons for Dom Alberic's accolade.

CHAPTER 7

Prayer

Communication with God

Prayer has to do with communication with God. This is the case even with what is called "silent prayer," because "like silence in music or a significant silence in conversation, [it] has meaning only in a context that can be heard and understood."[1] This communicative aspect of prayer is at its most obvious when a Christian prays verbally, speaks to God. In Macquarrie's understanding, and indeed here he represents the best of the Christian tradition, our human address to God in prayer is a situation in which God is already ahead of us, so to speak, taking the initiative: "...we must say of prayer... that God himself is its author. It is unitive Being (the Holy Spirit) that moves us to prayer, in response to the self-communication of Being, a communication that is possible because Being is immanent in every being."[2]

This takes us to the very heart of prayer. It is not something that we humans do in order to make God present to us. God is never absent. It is not something we do to make God aware of us and our needs. God is never unaware. Christian prayer, rather, is the mechanism in and through which God reaches out to creation, to the high point of creation in human persons, in order to give himself and to share his existence. There is an entelechy to human existence, to existence as such, and that consists in the divine transformation of what is begun in creation, definitively shaped in reconciliation, and is being brought to consummation, all in and through Jesus Christ, as expressive Being. Approached in this way prayer can never be understood as an entirely discrete action. It is not "some special department of life, but continuous with all our activities."[3] Macquarrie recognizes that this description of prayer may seem removed from the popular understanding and practice. He says: "We seem to be taking as the norm the prayers of saints and mystics, and ignoring prayer as it is commonly understood and practiced by ordinary Christians."[4] To avoid this charge and to root his understanding of prayer in the ordinary practices of the faithful, he turns his attention to petitionary prayer, perhaps the most common form of prayer.

Petitionary Prayer

Petitionary prayer is asking God for things, asking God to perform specific actions in the world. How does the view of prayer articulated above fit with petitionary prayer? Immediately it must be said that petitionary prayer has nothing to do with magic, with attempts to manipulate reality through occult means. Nor does genuine petitionary prayer have to do with egocentric prayer, prayer focused on the needs of the self, which "wither away when they are really brought before God and exposed to the judgment of Holy Being."[5] To avoid that kind of egocentricity petitionary prayer has to be consistent and continuous with the rest of life. Thus, "petitionary prayer makes sense if we are committing ourselves to what we are praying for, and if we can hold up this kind of commitment in the light of holy Being."[6] In this way petitionary prayer articulates appropriately the fundamental shape of the person's life, and is not a sort of "bolt from the blue."

What about the efficacy of petitionary prayer? Does it work? There is no doubt in Macquarrie's mind: "One may readily admit that (petitionary) prayer has repercussions beyond the life of the person or persons who actually offer the prayer."[7] Of course, it would be sheer hubris to attempt to measure in some quantifiable fashion the efficacy of prayer. That would reduce Mystery to mechanics. It is more a matter of acknowledging: God's holy permeative presence in creation, as well as his transcendence; human interconnectedness or communion; and the mysterious but powerful engagement of both. "Basically, it seems to me that intercessory prayer provides, as it were, openings into the dense texture of the human situation through which can come the creative and healing power of the reality we call God; and because within that human situation our lives are all bound together in a mysterious solidarity, then God's power is able to operate far beyond the particular person who offers the prayer, though through him. Prayer, as petition and intercession, helps to make the human person porous to the divine reality—the whole human reality, and not only that part of it actively engaged in prayer."[8] What a splendid passage! God's immanent presence is affirmed as foundational, but the human presence is not always and necessarily open to the divine. The human world is a "dense texture." It is, however, not a dense texture of discrete individuals, but of a communion of persons bound together "in mysterious solidarity." Prayer of petition makes the communion of persons "porous," permeable by the Divine Presence luring it into transformation. Thus, prayers are "answered."

Of course, what hinders the fulfilling of God's creative-reconciling-consummating love in his creatures is "the resistance offered by human wills, exercising their limited freedom to impede the work of creation-reconciliation-consummation."[9] Those who advance in the life of prayer know that it is their submission to and cooperation with the action of the Holy Spirit within them that constitutes this prayer, and not their own, individual, unaided effort. The more submission and cooperation is in place, then the more efficacious becomes the action of the Holy Spirit. Impediments are cleared out of the way.

Varieties of Spirituality

"The eucharist is the center of Christian prayer and worship, but it has become surrounded by many other acts of prayer and devotion. These are designed to extend the pattern of the eucharist into all of life."[10] Macquarrie's perspective here echoes that of Vatican

Council II's Constitution on the Sacred Liturgy. While the eucharist is the source and summit of Christian life, it must be supported and surrounded by other forms of prayer and devotion.[11] The primary focus of this eucharistic extension into the whole of life is the Liturgy of the Hours, but it is not the only form of prayer and spirituality.

Since every person is in some degree unique, "there must be many patterns of spirituality to suit the many needs and temperaments."[12] Throughout the sweep of the Christian tradition different types of spirituality have come into being, meeting the different needs and temperaments. However, within this great and legitimate plurality, "the vision itself is one and exercises a control over the plurality of spiritual disciplines."[13] There is a classic pattern to the vision.

The Shape of Christian Worship

"For the fundamental shape of Christian worship, we turn again to the eucharist, as the norm of such worship."[14] Throughout the Christian Churches which celebrate the eucharist as norm there is a certain ritual flexibility, but, at the same time, a definite threefold sequence is discernible: penitence, the ministry of the word, and the eucharist proper.

Penitence may involve, as in the Catholic Mass, a formal aspect as in the penitential part of the introductory rites. Confession of and sorrow for sin is made to God before the assembly moves on to the praise of God in the Gloria. Even in those churches whose liturgy is somewhat different, however, penitence ought to take place before participation in public worship in line with the Pauline recommendation in 1 Corinthians 11 about self-examination before receiving holy communion. In terms of the classic description of the spiritual life in the Christian tradition, penitence corresponds to what has been called "the purgative way."

The ministry of the Word is based on the appointed readings from Holy Scripture, the homily and the recitation of the creed. This corresponds to "the illuminative way," as the assembly hears the good news and renews and confirms its faith.

The eucharist proper, the consecration of the elements and the sharing in holy communion is best understood as "incorporation into the body of Christ." This corresponds in the classic schema to "the unitive way."

This classic eucharistic shape of Christian worship finds further expansion in the liturgical cycle of the Christian year.

> The penitential seasons of Advent and Lent lead the worshippers along the purgative way. The remembering and proclaiming of God's mighty acts in Christ and the new life which they open to mankind is the illuminative way that instructs and confirms the worshippers in faith. And the so-called "green Sundays" that follow the feasts of Whitsuntide and Trinity Sunday are the period of growth and sanctification when the unitive action of the Spirit builds up the church, so that we can speak of the unitive way.[15]

This approach of Macquarrie's is most helpful and expressive of eucharistic ecclesiology. The first axiom of eucharistic ecclesiology is that "the eucharist makes the church." The eucharist is the text that inscribes itself on the entire shape of the Christian's life. He puts it like this: "What we are saying then is that eucharistic worship compresses the Christian life into the action of the liturgy....Worship concentrates existence by creating selfhood and confirming the existent to Christ; and this process of conformation is promoted by the summing up in the act of worship of the form and order of the Christian life."[16] In some quarters today, even among Roman Catholic theologians, there is a suggestion that the eucharist no longer ought to enjoy this normative character and place in Christian life. The centrality of the eucharist is sometimes seen as an assumption of "Northern Hemisphere Catholicism," and to that extent as an imposition on the innate religiosity of non–Northern Hemisphere peoples and cultures.[17] This would negate the catholicity of the eucharist, eliminating its power as transcultural gift of unity. Macquarrie's perspective not only sees the eucharist as central and normative for Christianity as a whole but, indeed, as shaping the entirety of Christian prayer and life.

Comparison with Karl Rahner, S.J.

On John Macquarrie's desk in his home there is a framed photograph of himself and the late Karl Rahner, S.J., taken on the grounds of Christchurch College, the University of Oxford, just weeks before Rahner died. The picture frames not just the images of the two theologians, but also Macquarrie's relationship with Rahner. In the first edition of his *Principles of Christian Theology*, published in 1966, Macquarrie wrote:

> Among contemporary theologians I have found Karl Rahner the most helpful. In saying this, I am acknowledging that the leadership in theology, which even ten years ago lay with such Protestant giants as Barth, Brunner, and Tillich, has now passed to Roman Catholic thinkers. Among them, Karl Rahner (himself a penetrating student of Heidegger) is outstanding. He handles in a masterly way those tensions which constitute the peculiar dialectic of theology....[18]

In his earlier *Twentieth Century Religious Thought,* Macquarrie first acknowledges his interest in and awareness of Rahner's work.[19] In 1984, the last year of Rahner's life, for his eightieth birthday, Macquarrie gave a lecture in his presence at a symposium honoring him at Heythrop College, the University of London.[20] It makes sense to contrast Rahner's theology of prayer with Macquarrie's.

In an interview given on his seventy-fifth birthday, Rahner made these comments on his book *On Prayer:* "The little book *On Prayer* is…for me just as important as those more scholarly matters— even though it is 'only' a devotional book."[21] "Prayer is not easy. It is not the speaking of words or the hypnotic spell of the recited formula; it is the raising of the heart and mind to God in constantly renewed acts of love."[22]

Our lives are lived out within a certain context of ambiguity, that is, the quality of having more than one meaning. The meaning of life is not crystal clear to us. Such final and unmistakable clarity is available only in heaven.

> Only in heaven can [man] fully achieve [the] syntheses of all his faculties, of all the energies of his being, in the contemplation of the beatific vision. Here on earth, hedged in by the things of the senses, such synthesis is impossible...; and yet, in prayer, though "through a glass in a dark manner" [one] looks upon God and comes as near as he can to that unity of action and purpose for which [the] heart has a deep and secret longing.[23]

"Prayer is the opening of the heart to God,"[24] the God who is simply present to us, but there are obstacles to this opening. What obstacles? Rahner points to two: escapism and despair.

"Escapism" attempts to deal with the restlessness of the human heart by offering a way out, an exit from this restlessness, by saturating the heart in "debris." "Filling our lives in the same futility, frustration, monotony, chatter, and all that weary swirl of pointless striving we call human life."[25] "Despair," or what he terms "chronic despair," is settling for the apparent normalcy of self-control in life, self-direction, informed by societal expectations.

> Those who have settled down to this chronic despair preserve their self-control, appear to be leading—and regard themselves as leading—a perfectly natural life. They behave reasonably, work conscientiously, observe standards of decency, marry, found a settled home, discuss the arts and sciences. Occasionally, they like to indulge in a little speculation about the meaning and value of human life, or to listen to such speculation.[26]

It's all tantalizingly reasonable and normal and even desirable, but without prayer, this chronic despair is death-dealing. Behind it, says Rahner, lies "that wound from which the heart is bleeding to spiritual death."[27] Without the transforming awareness of God we die. So, we must "dig it out, so to speak, from under the refuse of the ordinary business of life."[28]

Both escapism and chronic despair fail because they are ultimately egocentric. The pulsing center is the self, the ego, and not God, and to that extent it is not only deficient but destructive. Instead of being *ego-centric,* the heart, to find genuine and lasting fulfillment must be *ec-centric,* that is, it must find its true center outside the self, in God. Rahner writes: "Yet, by a splendid paradox, it can be said that in ceasing to be himself the center of his life, he becomes more entirely one with himself; because God is more the true center of our being than we are ourselves. The sheer immensity of God urges us to realize our being to its fullest through transcending the limitations imposed by choosing to remain our own center."[29]

How then in practical terms is this eccentricity, this centeredness in God, achieved especially if one is unaccustomed to regular prayer? Rahner's answer is very straightforward, and amounts to saying, "Just do it!" Here are his words: "...[One] must take the initial step of laying aside...paralyzing anxiety. If [one] feels incapable of praying, he must nevertheless kneel, join his hands, speak words of prayer even if he feels that these words come only from his lips and that his heart remains unmoved."[30] The very discipline of "just doing it" is an effective step toward the opening of the heart to God.

For Rahner there is a profound sense in which this opening up of the heart cannot fail. It cannot fail because the very doing of it demonstrates our personal acknowledgment, however limited, that our hearts are restless and God is the *terminus a quo* and the *terminus ad quem* of the restlessness. Citing especially those famous words of Augustine, Rahner concludes:

> For deep in our hearts there is a profound restlessness, because God has given us a thirst for the infinite, for the

incomprehensible, for himself: "Thou hast made us for thy-self, O Lord...and our heart is restless until it rests in Thee." Deep in our buried heart, we find this seed of the divine, this restless reaching out toward something infinitely beyond the things of this world...."[31]

This restlessness in the human heart is not a human achieve-ment. It is not a restlessness created by human beings. It is just there. But it is more than just there. It is given with our existence. This restlessness for God is a gift from God:

A thirst for the infinite has been made part of the very essence of the human soul....The paradox here is that we must love God with a love implanted in us by God; for this love...is a free gift of God, beyond our power to achieve or to merit by our own unaided efforts....When, under the guidance of grace, we recognize this vague yearning as a thirst for infinity, for God, the love of God comes alive in our souls. Deeply implanted in human nature is a...longing for the God of his heart and the God who is his portion for ever.[32]

Reaching into (being reached into?) this deeply implanted long-ing for God brings the Christian to the brink of mystical experience. This is not mystical experience accompanied by all manner of spe-cial psycho-physical experiences. These for Rahner are secondary.

If we want to describe as "mysticism" this experience of transcendence in which man in the midst of ordinary life is always beyond himself and beyond the particular object with which he is concerned, we might say that mysticism always occurs, concealed and namelessly, in the midst of ordinary life and is the condition of the possibility for the most down-to-earth and most secular experience or ordi-nary life.[33]

This description of prayer by Rahner is not far removed from Macquarrie's. For both of them God is the author of prayer. God is the final satisfaction and fulfillment of the restlessness of the human heart. Prayer has absolutely nothing to do with magic or manipulation. Rather, it pulls the human person from within into deep alignment with God. For both the need of prayer is an anthropological constant that is ignored to the detriment of the human person. Prayer is awareness of and in that awareness responsiveness to the God in whom we live and move and have our being.

Doctors of Prayer

In his foreword to Rahner's autobiographical interview with Meinhold Krauss, Father Harvey Egan, S.J., calls Rahner, "Doctor Orationis," Doctor of Prayer.[34] I find myself wishing to make the same description of John Macquarrie. He too is a Doctor of Prayer. As with Rahner, not just Macquarrie's immediate writing on prayer but the entire corpus of his work is mystagogical, drawing us into the heart of the Mystery of Holy Being. Holy Being has poured itself out in creation, has entered human history, so as to make that history "the theater of God's unparalleled intimacy with the human person."[35] For Rahner and Macquarrie the central task of theology, and indeed, the ultimate goal of the entire Christian life is *reductio in mysterium*, being found through being led into the very heart of God.[36]

John Macquarrie at home in his study, 1998.

Conclusion

In recent years there have been various attempts to classify theologies and theologians according to a typology. Two of the more successful of these typologies have been constructed by David Tracy of Chicago and the late Hans Frei of Yale.[1] Sometimes people speak of a "Chicago School" and a "Yale School." Tracy stands for a correlational theology, yet a correlational theology that differs from Paul Tillich's. Crudely speaking, Tillich's correlational methodology moves through listening to the critical and existential questions raised by the culture and supplies the responses to these questions from the tradition of Christian faith. Tracy's approach moves beyond this. His method of correlation works out of a dual fidelity, a fidelity to the classics of the Christian tradition, with the Scriptures as the classics par excellence, and to contemporary experience. Contemporary experience for Tracy includes the wide range of modern and contemporary philosophies, engaged in a mutually critical correlation with the Christian classics. Frei, on the other hand, maintained that theologies which give philosophy a systematic priority inevitably distort Christian faith. Such theologies appear to permit reality to be defined in terms "external" to the biblical tradition. Where Tracy would be involved in an apologetic for the credibility and livability of Christianity, Frei would have suggested that Christianity's credibility and integrity could only be lived in its self-evident witness, not in reference to some set of extra-Christian criteria. The dialogue/debate between the two so called "schools" continues.

If we had to situate John Macquarrie in this context, he would be closer to David Tracy than to Hans Frei. Macquarrie works from general human experience to the data of Christian revelation and faith. Macquarrie's penchant is for something of Tracy's critical correlation between the classics of Christianity and public discourse, informed primarily for him by philosophy. Thus, his interest in Heidegger's contribution to theology has not abated, as is evidenced by his *Heidegger and Christianity*.[2] Yet, this does not do justice to Macquarrie's contribution. In an interesting essay entitled "Liberal and Radical Theologies Compared," Macquarrie writes, "The wisest theologians avoid getting themselves labelled too precisely."[3] While Macquarrie is more of a correlationist than a postliberal theologian in the Yale/Frei tradition, he is not easily labeled as a liberal or a radical. Indeed, in his defense of, for example, the Marian dogmas, some would describe him as a conservative theologian.

Macquarrie is best described in his own terms as a dialectical theologian, that is, a committed Christian theologian possessed of the skill to think dialectically in an habitual fashion. He establishes in his evenhandedness and fair treatment of others a real ability to enter into seemingly opposing systems of thought or points of view to see another aspect of the Christian mystery. His theology is not marked by "stifling absorption" in someone else's thought categories, nor by "damaging division" in relation to the positions of others. His theological perspective is above all marked by balance. One commentator on his theological method puts it like this: "The balance gives rise to a delicacy and harmony in his theology. Tensions seem not only held together but resolved; divergences and convergences of thought when taken together yield disclosures of God and of us....His balance serves to translate the peace of the Gospel from intellectual interpretations into feeling tones."[4] Anyone who has read deeply in Macquarrie would agree.

The Scottish Dominican theologian, Fergus Kerr, O.P., says that there is in Macquarrie a "total lack of *odium theologicum*."[5] That is quite an accomplishment. This correlational theologian, whose life is a lesson in real ecumenical conversion, has offered much to the church, to all the Christian churches, not least to Anglicanism and Catholicism. His way of doing theology offers all Christians a successful paradigm for this new century and millennium.

Notes

Chapter I. Introducing John Macquarrie

1. John Macquarrie, *Principles of Christian Theology,* rev. ed. (London: SCM Press, 1977), p. 1.

2. *Existence, Being and God: An Introduction to the Philosophical Theology of John Macquarrie* (New York: Paragon House, 1985), pp. 1–2.

3. The M.A. is the first degree in the Faculty of Arts in the University of Glasgow.

4. John Macquarrie, "Pilgrimage in Theology," in Alistair Kee and Eugene T. Long, ed., *Being and Truth: Essays in Honour of John Macquarrie* (London: SCM Press, 1986), p. xii.

5. Second edition edited by F. L. Cross and E. A. Livingstone (London and New York: Oxford University Press, 1974), p. 194.

6. In his *Twentieth Century Religious Thought: The Frontiers of Philosophy and Theology, 1900–1960* (London: SCM Press, 1963), p. 29.

7. F. H. Bradley, *The Principles of Logic,* 2nd ed., vol. 2 (London: Oxford University Press, 1922), pp. 688–89.

8. *Twentieth Century Religious Thought,* p. 29. See the brief but interesting description of Bradley in the article, "Macquarrie, John," in Alister E. McGrath, ed., *The SPCK Handbook of Anglican Theologians* (London: SPCK, 1998), p. 167.

9. *Twentieth Century Religious Thought,* pp. 34–35.

10. William B. Green, "Profile: John Macquarrie," *Epworth Review* 20 (1997): 13. I am much indebted to this fine article by Dr. Green.

11. *Paths in Spirituality,* rev. ed. (London: SCM Press, 1992), p. 107.

12. "Pilgrimage in Theology," p. xi.

13. London: SCM Press, 1952.

14. *An Existentialist Theology: A Comparison of Heidegger and Bultmann* (London: SCM Press), 1955, p. xi.

15. *Thinking About God* (London: SCM Press, 1975), p. 204.

16. New York: Charles Scribner's Sons, 1958.

17. Eugene T. Long in Eugene T. Long, ed., *God, Secularization and History: Essays in Memory of Ronald Gregor Smith* (Columbia, S.C.: University of South Carolina Press, 1974), p. vii.

18. Eugene T. Long, *Jaspers and Bultmann: A Dialogue Between Philosophy and Theology in the Existentialist Tradition* (Durham, N.C.: Duke University Press, 1968).

19. *A Century of Protestant Theology* (Philadelphia: Westminster Press, 1980), p. 126.

20. *The Doctrine of God* (Philadelphia: Westminster Press, 1970), p. 106.

21. *Thinking About God,* pp. 113–14; see also *God and Secularity* (Philadelphia: Westminster Press, 1967), pp. 23–25.

22. Clive L. Rawlins, *William Barclay: The Authorized Biography* (Grand Rapids: Eerdmans), 1984.

23. *God, Where Are You?* (London: Darton, Longman and Todd, 1997), pp. 117–18.

24. *Union Seminary Quarterly Review* 18 (1963); *Being and Time* (New York: Harper and Row, 1962).

25. New York: Harper and Row, 1963, p. 13.

26. *Existence, Being and God,* p. 10.

27. "Process and Faith, An American Testimony," in his *Thinking About God* (London: SCM Press, 1975), p. 215. The book is dedicated to Williams.

28. *In Search of Deity* (London: SCM Press, 1985), p. 146.

29. *Catholic Faith in a Process Perspective* (Maryknoll, N.Y.: Orbis Books, 1981), p. 20.

30. "Pilgrimage in Theology," p. xv, in John Knox, *The Church and the Reality of Chist* (New York: Harper and Row, 1962).

31. "Profile: John Macquarrie," p. 15.

32. From a letter to the author dated September 14, 1976.

33. "Profile: John Macquarrie," p. 16.

34. London: SCM Press, 1998, p. 7.

35. New York: Triumph Books, 1989, pp. 77–78.

36. In David F. Ford, ed., *The New Theologians,* vol. 2 (Oxford: Blackwell, 1989), pp. 30–72, with pp. 48–54 on Macquarrie.

37. Contemporary Theologians, p. 87.

38. *Apologetics and the Eclipse of Mystery: Mystagogy According to Karl Rahner* (Notre Dame and London: University of Notre Dame Press, 1980), p. xvi.

39. "British Theologies," p. 49. A similar criticism is expressed in the short but incisive article of Klauspeter Blaser and Pierre Gisel, "Macquarrie, John (1919–)," in Pierre Gisel, ed., *Encyclopédie du Protestantisme* (Paris: Editions du Cerf, 1995), p. 926.

40. Minneapolis: Winston Press, 1980, p. 19.

41. Frances M. Young, *Face to Face: A Narrative Essay in the Theology of Suffering* (Edinburgh: T. & T. Clark, 1990), pp. 56–57.

42. Cited from Humphrey Carpenter, *Robert Runcie, The Reluctant Archbishop* (London: Hodder and Stoughton, 1996), p. 88.

43. *Theology on Dover Beach* (London: Darton, Longman and Todd, 1979), p. 4.

44. *Journal of Theological Studies* 18 (1967): 292. The entire review runs from pp. 292–97.

45. Fergus Kerr, O.P., "Idealism and Realism: An Old Controversy Dissolved," in Kenneth Surin, ed., *Christ, Ethics and Tragedy: Essays in Honour of Donald Mackinnon* (Cambridge: Cambridge University Press, 1989), p. 16.

46. *Journal of Theological Studies* 29 (1978): 617.

47. The letter was kindly provided by Professor Macquarrie and is dated June 1, 1967.

48. *The Analogical Imagination* (New York: Crossroad, 1981).

49. "Incarnation as Root of the Sacramental Principle," in David Brown and Ann Loades, ed., *The Sacramental Word* (London: SPCK, 1996), p. 31.

50. *Le Métier de theologien: Entretiens avec G. Daix* (Paris: Editions France-Empire, 1979), p. 156.

Chapter 2. Speaking of God

1. See Allan D. Galloway, *Faith in a Changing Culture* (London: Allen and Unwin, 1968), pp. 51–63, especially p. 63.

2. See Bernard J. F. Lonergan, *Insight* (London: Longmans Green, 1958), chapter 10, and *Method in Theology* (New York: Herder and Herder, 1972), pp. 57–99.

3. "Fifty Years of Metaphysical Reflection: The Universe As Journey," in Gerald A. McCool, ed., *The Universe As Journey: Conversations with*

W. Norris Clarke, S.J. (New York: Fordham University Press, 1988), p. 50.

4. "Approaching the Christian Understanding of God," in Francis Schüssler Fiorenza and John P. Galvin, ed., *Systematic Theology: Roman Catholic Perspectives*, vol. 1 (Minneapolis: Fortress Press, 1991), p. 134.

5. *Existence, Being and God* (New York: Paragon House, 1985), pp. 37–38.

6. Ibid., p. 39.

7. *Principles of Christian Theology*, p. 110.

8. *Being and Time*, trans. J. Macquarrie and E. Robinson (New York: Harper and Row, 1962), p. 62.

9. Herbert McCabe, O.P., *God Matters* (London: Geoffrey Chapman, 1987), especially pp. 2–9, 39–51.

10. *God-Talk*, pp. 99–100.

11. Cited in *God-Talk*, p. 82.

12. Ibid., p. 100; *Thinking About God*, p. 106.

13. Cited in Eugene T. Long, *Existence, Being and God*, p. 41.

14. *Our Experience of God* (London: Allen and Unwin, 1959), p. 40.

15. *Theology and Metaphysics* (London: SCM Press, 1970), p. 112.

16. *The Concept of God* (Oxford: Blackwell, 1974), p. 139.

17. Ibid., p. 150.

18. *God and Secularity*, p. 107.

19. *Thinking About God*, p. 107.

20. ST Ia, q. 13, art. 11. See *God-Talk*, p. 100.

21. *Theology on Dover Beach* (London: Darton, Longman and Todd, 1979), p. 30.

22. Eugene T. Long, *Existence, Being and God*, p. 49.

23. See the positive comments of the Methodist liturgical and ecumenical theologian Geoffrey Wainwright in his *Doxology, A Systematic Theology* (New York and Oxford: Oxford University Press, 1980), pp. 350–51, a book dedicated to Macquarrie.

24. David Tracy, *The Analogical Imagination*, p. 145. In fact, in this essay, in the section dealing with this alternative model of perfection, Tracy refers to Macquarrie's *In Search of Deity* as "an important study."

25. See his *Concepts of Deity* (New York: Herder and Herder, 1971), especially pp. 131–51. Similar critical remarks are made of

Notes

Macquarrie by Illtyd Trethowan, O.S.B., in *Absolute Value: A Study in Christian Theism* (London: Allen and Unwin, 1970), pp. 170–77, and by Maurice Curtin, "God's Presence in the World: The Metaphysics of Aquinas and Some Recent Thinkers—Moltmann, Macquarrie, Rahner," in Fran O'Rourke, ed., *At the Heart of the Real: Philosophical Essays in Honour of Desmond Connell* (Dublin: Irish Academic Press, 1992), pp. 123–36.

26. Eugene T. Long, *Existence, Being and God,* p. 50.

27. *The God We Never Knew* (San Francisco: Harper Collins, 1997), pp. 12, 30–33.

28. *In Search of Deity,* p. 54.

29. John Macquarrie, "Incarnation as Root of the Sacramental Principle," in David Brown and Ann Loades, ed., *Christ: The Sacramental Word* (London: SPCK, 1996), p. 31.

30. *In Search of Deity,* p. 171.

31. This is how it is put in his description of Macquarrie by the Irish systematic theologian, Denis Carroll, *A Pilgrim God for a Pilgrim People* (Dublin: Gill and Macmillan, 1988), p. 143.

32. *The Grain of Wheat,* trans. E. Leiva-Merikakis (San Francisco: Ignatius Press, 1995), p. 2.

33. London: Macmillan, 1934, p. 478.

34. *In Search of Deity,* p. 181. The Irish systematic theologian, Gerard O'Hanlon, S.J., in his fine study, *The Immutability of God in the Theology of Hans Urs von Balthasar* (Cambridge: Cambridge University Press, 1990), p. 212, seems to misunderstand Macquarrie as positing an almost unqualified, univocal passibility in God. O'Hanlon bases his judgment on his reading of Macquarrie's *The Humility of God* but has not taken account of the later Gifford Lectures, *In Search of Deity.*

35. "A New Look at the Immutability of God," in Robert Roth, ed., *God Knowable and Unknowable* (New York: Fordham University Press, 1973), pp. 43–72.

36. Review of *In Search of Deity,* in *New Blackfriars* (1984), pp. 439–40. For a perceptive and sensitive understanding of Macquarrie's own appreciation of Thomism, see his *Twentieth Century Religious Thought,* pp. 278–300, and his essay on the premier Anglican Thomist of the last century, Eric L. Mascall, "Mascall and Thomism," *The Tufton Review* 1 (1998): 1–13.

37. *The God of Jesus Christ,* trans. M. J. O'Connell (London: SCM Press, 1983), p. 295.

38. Nicholas Lash, "Considering the Trinity," *Modern Theology* 2 (1986): 183, an essay to which I am much indebted. Lash refers to Swinburne's *The Coherence of Christian Theism* (Oxford: Clarendon Press, 1977) as exemplifying what Kasper calls the "heresy of Christian theism," but perhaps he overlooks Swinburne's very considerable contributions as a Christian apologist.

39. *Principles of Christian Theology,* p. 193.

40. *The Three-Personed God: The Trinity as a Mystery of Salvation* (Washington, D.C.: The Catholic University of America Press, 1982), pp. 146–47.

41. St. Augustine, *The Trinity,* V.10, trans. E. Hill (Brooklyn, N.Y.: New City Press, 1991), p. 196.

42. *Principles of Christian Theology,* p. 194.

43. Ibid., p. 198.

44. Ibid., pp. 199–200.

45. *She Who Is: The Mystery of God in Feminist Theological Discourse* (New York: The Crossroad Publishing Company, 1992), p. 210. Note also her approving comments on Macquarrie on pp. 239, 251.

Chapter 3. Knowing Jesus Christ

1. London: SCM Press, 1998.

2. Wickham's review of *Christology Revisited* is aptly entitled "Hold That Paradox," *Church Times,* November 7, 1998, p. 20.

3. In his *Mary for All Christians* (London: Collins, 1990), p. 120.

4. *Christology Revisited,* p. 17.

5. *Christology Revisited,* p. 18. Macquarrie acknowledges that he has been described as an adoptionist, though he believes it an unjust description. He does not tell us who his critics are, but the charge was leveled by Charles C. Hefling of Boston College in his article, "Reviving Adamic Adoptionism: The Example of John Macquarrie," *Theological Studies* 52 (1991).

6. *Christology Revisited,* p. 32.

7. John McIntyre, review of John Macquarrie, *Christology Revisited; The Expository Times* 111 (1999): 265. There is an excellent and full critical account of Macquarrie's Christology in McIntyre's *The Shape of Christology,* 2nd ed. (Edinburgh: T. & T. Clark, 1996), pp. 259–82.

8. *Christology Revisited,* p. 34.

9. Ibid., p. 35.

10. *Jesus Christ in Modern Thought* (London: SCM Press, 1990), pp. 393–94.

11. *Christology Revisited,* p. 37.

12. Ibid., p. 40.

13. *Principles of Christian Theology,* rev. ed. (London: SCM Press, 1977), p. 289.

14. *Christian Hope* (New York: Seabury, 1978), p. 74.

15. Ibid., p. 72; *Principles of Christian Theology,* p. 288.

16. Ibid.

17. *The Faith of the People of God* (London: SCM Press, 1972), p. 63.

18. *Christian Hope,* p. 76.

19. *Jesus Risen* (London: Darton, Longman and Todd, 1987), p. 27.

20. *Christian Hope,* p. 76.

21. *The Humility of God* (London: SCM Press, 1978,) p. 79.

22. *Principles of Christian Theology,* p. 305.

23. *Christian Hope,* pp. 80–81.

24. *Christology Revisited,* p. 62.

25. *The Expository Times* 77 (1966): 199–200. There is an excellent discussion of Macquarrie's use of the findings of New Testament scholarship on the pre-existence of Christ in Pauline and Johannine texts in Niall Coll, *Some Anglican Interpretations of Christ's pre-Existence: A Study of L. S. Thornton, E. L. Mascall, J. A. T. Robinson and J. Macquarrie* (Rome: Gregorian University Press, 1995), pp. 190–208.

26. *Jesus Christ in Modern Thought,* pp. 391–92.

27. *Christology* (Oxford and New York: Oxford University Press, 1995), p. 238.

28. Ibid., pp. 242–43.

29. *Christology Revisited,* p. 59.

30. *Jesus Christ in Modern Thought,* p. 213; Niall Coll, in *Some Anglican Interpretations of Christ's pre-Existence,* p. 182, maintains that "Macquarrie, in adopting this position, is aligning himself with the general thrust of post-Enlightenment thought and rejecting one of the main planks in the metaphysics of classical Christology." That is

not unfair provided one does not reach the unwarranted conclusion that Macquarrie is uncritical of the Enlightenment.

31. "Revisiting the Christological Dimensions of Uniqueness," in Leonard Swidler and Paul Mojzes, ed., *The Uniqueness of Jesus: A Dialogue with Paul Knitter* (Maryknoll, N.Y.: Orbis Books, 1997), p. 94. Here Macquarrie's position is presented without specific reference to Knitter.

32. Ibid., p. 96.

33. John Macquarrie, *Mediators Between Human and Divine, From Moses to Muhammad* (New York: Continuum, 1996), p. 148.

34. The quotation is from *De Incarnatione* 41, cited in *Mediators Between Human and Divine,* p. 148. St. Athanasius has remained a special interest of Macquarrie's, as Alistair Kee points out in his *The Way of Transcendence* (Harmondsworth: Penguin Books, 1971), p. 55. See *Studies in Christian Existentialism* (London: SCM Press, 1965), pp. 221ff., and *God-Talk* (London: SCM Press, 1967), pp. 123–46.

35. John Macquarrie, "Incarnation," in Alister E. McGrath, ed., *The Blackwell Encyclopedia of Modern Christian Thought* (Oxford: Basil Blackwell, 1993), p. 269.

36. "Revisiting the Christological Dimensions of Uniqueness," pp. 97–98.

37. *In Search of Humanity* (London: SCM Press, 1982), p. 67.

38. *Christology Revisited,* pp. 86, 95–97.

39. Ibid., p. 91.

40. Ibid., p. 92. He goes on to add, "I hasten to say that I myself am not a mystic. I have admired the river from the banks and dabbled in the shallows, but I have never had the courage to plunge into the depths." It seems to me that this is the characteristic of the man, because his sense of God's presence is so complete that it is not adequately described in anything less than mystical terms.

41. Ibid., p. 106.

42. Francesca A. Murphy, *Christ the Form of Beauty* (Edinburgh: T. & T. Clark, 1995), pp. 176–78, 180–83.

Chapter 4. Church and Sacrament

1. Cited in Paul McPartlan, *Sacrament of Salvation* (Edinburgh: T. & T. Clark, 1995), p. xiii.

2. John Macquarrie, *On Being a Theologian: Reflections at Eighty* (London: SCM Press, 1999), p. 38.

3. *Principles of Christian Theology,* rev. ed. (London: SCM Press, 1977), p. 386.

4. Ibid., pp. 388, 407.

5. As noted in chapter 1, Knox was Macquarrie's friend and colleague at Union Theological Seminary in New York City. Macquarrie quotes this phrase from Knox's book, *The Church and the Reality of Christ,* p. 104.

6. *Principles of Christian Theology,* p. 389.

7. Ibid., p. 390.

8. Ibid., p. 402.

9. Ibid., p. 403. The same point is made in *Christian Unity and Christian Diversity* (London: SCM Press, 1975), p. 47.

10. John D. Zizioulas, *Being as Communion: Studies in Personhood and the Church* (London: Darton, Longman and Todd, 1985); Jean-Marie R. Tillard, O.P., *Church of Churches* (Collegeville, Minn.: Liturgical Press, 1992).

11. *Principles of Christian Theology,* p. 405.

12. *Epiphany: A Theological Introduction to Catholicism* (Collegeville, Minn.: Liturgical Press, 1996), p. 237.

13. *Principles of Christian Theology,* p. 407.

14. Ibid., p. 409.

15. Ibid., p. 410.

16. Ibid.

17. Ibid., p. 411.

18. Hans Kung, ed., *Post-Ecumenical Christianity* (New York: Herder and Herder, 1970), pp. 45–46.

19. *Principles of Christian Theology,* p. 416.

20. These last three observations about Peter come from Macquarrie's essay, "The Papacy in a Unified Church," in his *On Being a Theologian: Reflections at Eighty,* pp. 163–64.

21. *Principles of Christian Theology,* p. 413.

22. Ibid., p. 415. This is a favorite analogy for Macquarrie. He returns to it again in his essay, "The Papacy in a Unified Church," *On Being a Theologian,* p. 170.

23. "Structures of Unity," in Mark Santer, ed., *Their Lord and Ours: Approaches to Authority, Community and the Unity of the Church* (London: SPCK, 1982), p. 126.

24. *Christian Unity and Christian Diversity,* pp. 99–100.

25. *On Being a Theologian,* p. 169

26. Macquarrie finds particularly helpful Butler's "Roman Requirements," *The Tablet,* July 5, 1975, pp. 99–100.

27. *On Being a Theologian,* pp. 170–71.

28. Eamonn Conway, "The Papacy in a Pilgrim Church: Response to Prof. John Macquarrie," *On Being a Theologian,* p. 175.

29. *Christian Unity and Christian Diversity,* p. 99.

30. *On Being a Theologian,* p. 164. Macquarrie's positive comments on the papacy are mentioned by J. Michael Miller, C.S.B., in *The Divine Right of the Papacy in Recent Ecumenical Theology* (Rome: Gregorian University Press, 1980), pp. 125, 127, 133–34.

31. See his "Structures of Unity," in Mark Santer, ed., *Their Lord and Ours: Approaches to Authority, Community and the Unity of the Church* (London: SPCK, 1982), pp. 113–28.

32. Ibid., p. 119.

33. *Christian Unity and Christian Diversity,* p.17.

34. Ibid., p. 19.

35. Lesslie Newbigin, "All in One Place or All of One Sort? On Unity and Diversity in the Church," Richard W. A. McKinney, ed., *Creation, Christ and Culture: Studies in Honour of T. F. Torrance* (Edinburgh: T. & T. Clark, 1976), p. 293.

36. Ibid., p. 299.

37. John Macquarrie, "A Modern Scottish Theologian," in his collection *Thinking About God* (London: SCM Press, 1975), pp. 210–11.

38. John Macquarrie, *A Guide to the Sacraments* (New York: Continuum, 1997).

39. Ibid., p. viii.

40. London: SCM Press, 1972, pp. 98–99.

41. *A Guide to the Sacraments,* p. 6.

42. London: SCM Press, 1978, pp. 3–5.

43. *A Guide to the Sacraments*, p. 8.

44. New York: Catholic Book Publishing Co., 1994, no. 1117, pp. 289–90.

45. *A Guide to the Sacraments*, p. 37.

46. New York: Charles Scribner's Sons, 1972, pp. 127–28.

47. See his *Invitation to Faith* (Harrisburg, Pa.: Morehouse Publishing, 1995), p. 61.

48. *The Christian Sacraments* (London: Nisbet, 1927), p. 105. In the entry under his name in *The Oxford Dictionary of the Christian Church*, Quick is described in this fashion: "His approach to doctrinal issues was systematic and synthetic rather than historical, and essentially modern in expression" (2nd ed., Oxford: Oxford University Press, 1974, p. 1151). Though he is arguably more historically sensitive and aware than Quick, this could stand as a description of Macquarrie himself.

49. *Christian Unity and Christian Diversity*, p. 63.

50. Cited in Robert Hale, *Canterbury and Rome, Sister Churches* (New York/Mahwah, N.J.: Paulist Press, 1982), p. 16.

51. See *The Tablet*, June 10, 2000, p. 806.

52. See, for example, his essay, "Baptism, Confirmation, Eucharist," in J. Greenhalgh and E. Russell, ed., *Faith, Hope and Love* (London: St. Mary's, Bourne St., 1987), pp. 57–70.

53. *A Guide to the Sacraments*, p. 84.

54. *The Reconciliation of a Penitent* (London: General Synod of the Church of England, 1987).

55. Pp. 483–85.

56. *A Guide to the Sacraments*, p. 98.

57. Ibid., p. 93.

58. *A Guide to the Sacraments*, pp. 165–66.

59. *Principles of Christian Theology*, p. 486.

60. In this respect Macquarrie draws freely upon the work of the little known Oxford philosopher, and his colleague, John Lucas, "Notes on the Doctrine of a Metaphysical *Vinculum*," *Theology* (May 1975). Given the date of Lucas's article, it does not feature in his treatment of marriage in *Principles*, but it is there in Macquarrie's *Christian*

Unity and Christian Diversity, pp. 87–88, and in *A Guide to the Sacraments,* pp. 223–25.

61. *A Guide to the Sacraments,* p. 224.

62. *Principles of Christian Theology,* pp. 513–14.

63. *A Guide to the Sacraments,* p. 197.

64. Ibid., p. 180.

65. Ibid., p. 182.

66. Harrisburg, Pa.: Morehouse Publishing, 1993, p. 1.

67. *The Panther and the Hind* (Edinburgh: T. & T. Clark, 1993), p. 128.

68. *The Tablet,* September 20, 1997, p. 1197.

69. *Theology, Church and Ministry* (London: SCM Press, 1986), p. 107.

70. Hans Kung, ed., *Post-Ecumenical Christianity,* p. 53.

Chapter 5. The Eucharist

1. John Macquarrie, *A Guide to the Sacraments* (New York: Continuum, 1997), p. 102.

2. Rev. ed., Harrisburg, Pa.: Morehouse Publishing, 1992, p. 73.

3. *Christian Unity and Christian Diversity* (London: SCM Press, 1975), p. 66. In this respect it is helpful to note what Macquarrie has to say about heresy. See his *Thinking About God* (London: SCM Press, 1975), pp. 44–51.

4. *Principles of Christian Theology,* rev. ed. (London: SCM Press, 1977), p. 469. Most of Macquarrie's writing on the eucharist, while it pre-dates the Lima Statement of the Faith and Order Commission of the World Council of Churches in 1982 *(Baptism, Eucharist and Ministry),* is perfectly consistent with the eucharistic theology to be found there.

5. *Principles of Christian Theology,* p. 470.

6. In his essay, "Structures for Unity," in Mark Santer, ed., *Their Lord and Ours* (London: SPCK, 1982), p. 123.

7. London: SCM Press, 1990, p. 68. This is also the basis of his treatment, though with a gloss on traditional Anglican positions such as that of Cranmer, in his *A Guide to the Sacraments,* pp. 135–45.

8. *The Humility of God* (London: SCM Press, 1978), p. 5.

9. Ibid.

10. Ibid., pp. 425–26.

Notes

11. *Theology, Church and Ministry* (London: SCM Press, 1986), p. 176.

12. Hanson provides a fine account of the traditional evangelical Anglican criticism of eucharistic sacrifice in his *Christian Priesthood Examined* (London: Lutterworth Press, 1979) and, more extensively, in his *Eucharistic Offering in the Early Church* (Bramcote, Notts: Grove Books, 1979). Rowan Williams's equally fine reply to Hanson is his *Eucharistic Sacrifice: The Roots of a Metaphor* (Bramcote, Notts: Grove Books, 1982), pp. 24–33 are particularly outstanding.

13. *Eucharistic Offering in the Early Church,* p. 26.

14. *Eucharistic Sacrifice, The Roots of a Metaphor,* p. 2.

15. In a letter dated June 12, 1999.

16. *Paths in Spirituality,* rev. ed., p. 83.

17. Ibid.

18. *Principles of Christian Theology,* p. 474.

19. Ibid., pp. 449–50.

20. Ibid., p. 477.

21. *Paths in Spirituality,* p. 85.

22. Ibid., p. 86.

23. London: Macmillan, 1924. See *A Guide to the Sacraments,* pp. 132–33.

24. *Christian Unity and Christian Diversity,* p. 72.

25. *Paths in Spirituality,* p. 88.

26. *Principles of Christian Theology,* p. 478.

27. *Christian Unity and Christian Diversity,* p. 75. Macquarrie's citation is in Latin, and the English translation here is taken from Joseph Neuner, S.J. and Jacques Dupuis, S.J., ed., *The Christian Faith in the Doctrinal Documents of the Catholic Church,* rev. ed. (London: Collins, 1983), p. 15.

28. *Christian Unity and Christian Diversity,* pp. 75–76. Again, Macquarrie cites the Latin. The translation here is my own.

29. Ibid., p. 76.

30. Ibid., p. 88.

31. Ibid.

32. Ibid.

33. *Principles of Christian Theology,* p. 479.

34. *Christian Unity and Christian Diversity,* p. 73.

35. See Lindbeck's *The Nature of Doctrine* (Philadelphia: Westminster Press, 1984).

36. *Principles of Christian Theology,* p. 480.

37. *Paths in Spirituality,* p. 87.

38. F. L. Cross and P. E. More, *Anglicanism* (London: SPCK, 1951, p. 464).

39. *Paths in Spirituality,* p. 92.

40. *Christian Unity and Christian Diversity,* pp. 68–69.

41. Ibid., p. 71.

42. Ibid. See also Nathan Mitchell, *Cult and Controversy: The Worship of the Eucharist Outside the Mass* (New York: Pueblo Publishing Company, 1982), p. 417.

43. *Theology, Church and Ministry,* p. 185.

44. In his *Who's Who in Theology?* (New York: Crossroad, 1992), p. 81.

Chapter 6. Mary

1. George H. Tavard, *The Thousand Faces of the Blessed Virgin* (Collegeville, Minn.: Liturgical Press, 1996), pp. 134–52.

2. See his *The Joy of All Creation: An Anglican Meditation on the Place of Mary* (Cambridge, Mass.: Cowley Publications, 1985).

3. Austin Flannery, O.P., ed., *Vatican Council II: The Conciliar and Postconciliar Documents* (New York: Costello Publishing Company, 1975), pp. 413–23.

4. Ibid., par. 53, p. 414.

5. Ibid., par. 60, p. 418.

6. Ibid., par. 68, p. 422.

7. Geoffrey Wainwright, *Is the Reformation Over? Catholics and Protestants at the Turn of the Millennia* (Milwaukee: Marquette University Press, 2000), p. 53.

8. Raymond E. Brown, S.S., and others, ed., *Mary in the New Testament* (New York: Paulist Press, 1978).

9. The phrase is Elizabeth Johnson's in her article, "Mary, Contemporary Issues," in Wolfgang Beinert and Francis Schüssler Fiorenza, ed., *Handbook of Catholic Theology* (New York: Crossroad, 1995), p. 460.

10. All of the chapters, with the exception of chapter 4, of Macquarrie's *Mary for All Christians* (London: Collins, 1990), began as papers for the Ecumenical Society of the Blessed Virgin Mary.

11. *Christian Unity and Christian Diversity* (London: SCM Press, 1975), p. 90.

12. New York: Crossroad, 1999.

13. New York: Routledge, 1995.

14. San Francisco: Harper and Row, 1979.

15. *Principles of Christian Theology,* rev. ed., p. 393.

16. Ibid., rev. ed., London: SCM Press, 1977, p. 392.

17. Ibid., p. 393. For an approach to the historical Mary, see Owen F. Cummings, "The Real Mary of Nazareth," *The Priest* 48 (1992): 14–17.

18. *Principles of Christian Theology,* p. 395.

19. Ibid., p. 396.

20. Ibid., p. 397.

21. Ibid., p. 394; *Mary for All Christians,* pp. 46–47.

22. *Principles of Christian Theology,* p. 395.

23. Ibid., p. 397.

24. *Christian Unity and Christian Diversity,* p. 93.

25. Ibid.

26. Ibid., p. 94; *Mary for All Christians,* pp. 66–67.

27. *Principles of Christian Theology,* p. 398.

28. *Mary for All Christians,* pp. 81–82.

29. Ibid., p. 84.

30. Ibid., p. 91.

31. London: SCM Press, 1996. Pittenger said of this book, "This is my last book...." (p. ix).

32. R. A. Norris, ed., *Lux in Lumine: Essays to Honor W. Norman Pittenger* (New York: Seabury Press, 1966), p. 2.

33. *Our Lady,* pp. 2-22.

34. Ibid., p. 10.

35. Ibid., p. 14.

36. Ibid., p. 28, my emphasis. See also p. 54.

37. "Theology and Self-Awareness," in Alec R. Vidler, ed., *Soundings* (Cambridge: Cambridge University Press, 1963), p. 101.

38. Ibid., p. 25.

39. Ibid.

40. Ibid., p. 26.

41. For a more detailed critical appreciation of Pittenger see Owen F. Cummings, "A Critical Note on Norman Pittenger's Mariology," *New Blackfriars* 78 (1997): 336–40.

42. *Mary for All Christians*, p. xi.

Chapter 7. Prayer

1. John Macquarrie, *Principles of Christian Theology*, rev. ed. (London: SCM Press, 1977), p. 493.

2. Ibid., p. 494.

3. Ibid.

4. Ibid., p. 495.

5. Ibid.

6. Ibid., p. 496.

7. Ibid.

8. John Macquarrie, *Paths in Spirituality*, rev. ed. (Harrisburg, Pa.: Morehouse Publishing, 1992), pp. 27–28.

9. Ibid.

10. *Principles of Christian Theology*, p. 497.

11. Austin Flannery, O.P., ed., *Vatican Council II: The Conciliar and Postconciliar Documents* (New York: Costello, 1975), pp. 6–7.

12. *Principles of Christian Theology*, p. 498.

13. Ibid., p. 499.

14. Ibid., p. 500.

15. Ibid., p. 501. For a perspective similar to Macquarrie's, but treating of the eucharistic pattern in the cycle of psychological and faith development, see Owen F. Cummings, "Eucharist, Life-Cycle, Prayer," *Emmanuel* 104 (1998): 203–13.

16. *Principles*, p. 501.

17. For example, see Owen F. Cummings, "Is the Mass Eurocentric? A Response to Gary Riebe-Estrella," *Antiphon, A Journal for Liturgical Renewal* 4 (1999): 5–7.

Notes

18. *Principles of Christian Theology* (London: SCM Press, 1966), p. vii.

19. London: SCM Press, 1963, pp. 293–94.

20. "The Anthropological Approach to Theology," in his *Theology, Church and Ministry* (London: SCM Press, 1986), pp. 48–68.

21. Collegeville, Minn.: Liturgical Press, 1993.

22. Ibid., p. 9.

23. Ibid., p. 8.

24. Ibid., p. 10.

25. Ibid., p. 12.

26. Ibid., p. 13.

27. Ibid.

28. Karl Rahner, "Experience of the Holy Spirit," in *Theological Investigations* 18 (New York: Crossroad, 1983), p. 202.

29. Ibid., p. 18.

30. Ibid., p. 19.

31. Ibid., p. 21.

32. Ibid., pp. 39–48.

33. Karl Rahner, "Experience of the Holy Spirit," p. 197.

34. *Karl Rahner, I Remember: Autobiographical Interview with Meinhold Krauss* (New York: Crossroad, 1984), p. 11.

35. Geffrey B. Kelly, ed., *Karl Rahner: Theologian of the Graced Search for Meaning* (Minneapolis: Fortress Press, 1992), p. 59.

36. See R. R. Reno, *The Ordinary Transformed: Karl Rahner and the Christian Vision of Transcendence* (Grand Rapids: Eerdmans, 1995), pp. 219–22.

Conclusion

1. David Tracy, *Blessed Rage for Order: The New Pluralism in Theology* (New York: Seabury Press, 1975; reprinted with a new preface by the University of Chicago Press, 1996). Other key works by Tracy include: *The Analogical Imagination* (New York: Crossroad, 1981), *Plurality and Ambiguity* (Chicago and London: University of Chicago and London: University of Chicago Press, 1987), and *On Naming the Present: God, Hermeneutics and Church* (Maryknoll, N.Y.: Orbis Books, 1994). For Hans Frei see *Types of Christian Theology* (New Haven and London: Yale University Press, 1992), *The Identity of Jesus Christ: The Hermeneutical Bases of Dogmatic Theology*

(Philadelphia: Fortress Press, 1975), and the posthumously published *Theology and Narrative: Selected Essays,* ed., G. Hunsinger and W. C. Placher (New York: Oxford University Press, 1993).

2. London: SCM Press, 1994.

3. *Thinking About God* (London: SCM Press, 1975), 61.

4. J. J. Mueller, *What Are They Saying About Theological Method?* (New York/Ramsey, N.J.: Paulist Press, 1984), p. 27. See also Marion L. Hendrickson, *Behold the Man! An Anthropological Comparison of the Christologies of John Macquarrie and of Wolfhart Pannenberg* (Lanham/New York/Oxford: University Press of America, 1998), pp. 92–95, and David Jenkins, *The Scope and Limits of John Macquarrie's Existential Theology* (Uppsala: Acta Universitatis Upsaliensis, 1987), pp. 107–25.

5. Review of Alistair Kee and Eugene T. Long, ed., *Being and Truth: Essays in Honour of John Macquarrie,* and John Macquarrie, *Theology, Church and Ministry,* in *New Blackfriars* 68 (1987): 420.

Bibliography

The major books of John Macquarrie cited in the text.

(A complete bibliography may be found in his *On Being a Theologian*.)

An Existentialist Theology, A Comparison of Heidegger and Bultmann. London: SCM Press, 1955.

God-Talk: An Examination of the Language and Logic of Theology. London: SCM Press, 1962.

Twentieth Century Religious Thought. London: SCM Press, 1963. Rev. eds. 1971, 1981, 2001.

Principles of Christian Theology. London: SCM Press, 1966. Rev. ed., 1977.

God and Secularity. London: Lutterworth, 1967.

Three Issues in Ethics. New York: Harper and Row, 1970.

Paths in Spirituality. London: SCM Press, 1972. Rev. ed., 1992.

The Faith of the People of God: A Lay Theology. London: SCM Press, 1972.

Thinking About God. London: SCM Press, 1975.

Christian Unity and Christian Diversity. London: SCM Press, 1975.

Christian Hope. London: SCM Press, 1978.

The Humility of God. London: SCM Press, 1978.

In Search of Humanity. London: SCM Press, 1982.

John Macquarrie, a Master of Theology

Theology, Church and Ministry. London: SCM Press, 1986.

In Search of Deity. London: SCM Press, 1985.

Jesus Christ in Modern Thought. London: SCM Press, 1990.

Mary for All Christians. London: Collins, 1990.

Heidegger and Christianity. London: SCM Press, 1994.

Invitation to Faith. Harrisburg, Pa.: Morehouse Publishing, 1995.

Mediators Between Human and Divine: From Moses to Muhammad. New York: Continuum, 1996.

A Guide to the Sacraments. New York: Continuum, 1997.

Christology Revisited London: SCM Press, 1998.

On Being a Theologian: Reflections at Eighty. Ed. John H. Morgan. London: SCM Press, 1999.

Studies of John Macquarrie's Theology.

Coll, Niall. *Some Anglican Interpretations of Christ's pre-Existence: A Study of L. S. Thornton, E. L. Mascall, J. A. T. Robinson and J. Macquarrie.* Rome: Gregorian University Press, 1995.

Green, William B. "Profile: John Macquarrie." *Epworth Review* 20 (1997).

Kee, Alistair, and Eugene T. Long, eds. *Being and Truth: Essays in Honour of John Macquarrie.* London: SCM Press, 1986.

Long, Eugene T. *Being and God: An Introduction to the Philosophical Theology of John Macquarrie.* New York: Paragon House Publishers, 1985.

Morley, Georgina. *The Grace of Being: John Macquarrie's Natural Theology.* Bristol, Ind.: Wyndham Hall Press, 2001.

Index